MIDDLETOWN

GARLAND REFERENCE I
OF SOCIAL SCIENCE
(Vol. 446)

MIDDLETOWN
An Annotated Bibliography

David C. Tambo,
Dwight W. Hoover
and
John D. Hewitt

GARLAND PUBLISHING, INC. • NEW YORK & LONDON
1988

Library of Congress Cataloging-in-Publication Data
Tambo, David C.
Middletown: an annotated bibliography / David C. Tambo, Dwight W.
Hoover, and John D. Hewitt.
p. cm.—(Garland reference library of social science; vol.
446)
Includes index.
ISBN 0–8240–5839–9 (alk. paper)
1. Muncie (Ind.)—Social conditions—Bibliography.   2. Muncie
(Ind.)—Social life and customs—Bibliography.   3. Lynd, Robert
Staughton, 1892– Middletown—Bibliography.   4. Lynd, Helen
Merrell, 1896– —Bibliography.   I. Hoover, Dwight W., 1926– .
II. Hewitt, John D., 1945– .   III. Ball State University.   Center
for Middletown Studies.   IV. Title.   V. Series.

Z7165.U6I68   1988   [HN80.M85]   016.306′09772′65—dc19
87–34582   CIP

Printed on acid-free, 250-year-life paper
Manufactured in the United States of America

CONTENTS

PREFACE

In 1937 Robert Staughton and Helen Merrell Lynd published the second of their seminal Middletown studies. Half a century later, their work continues to be replicated and references to the Middletown studies permeate social science literature. This bibliography brings together all major, Middletown-related printed sources and dissertations known to the authors. It omits those references which mention the Middletown work of the Lynds and their successors only in passing. It also does not include publications by the Lynds which lack Middletown content.

Entries in this bibliography are arranged chronologically, beginning with local reaction to the Lynds' initial research in 1924 and ending with publications from mid-1987. We have chosen a chronological organization of material because it best shows the historical progression of Middletown studies. As a result, the findings and critical response to the work of a specific project such as Middletown III or the Middletown Film Series, tend to be grouped together and facilitate access for the reader. When there are several entries for the same date, arrangement is alphabetical by author's surname.

Many of the entries are from Muncie newspapers and illustrate vividly the effect of extended research upon a community. Middletown references have been collected by research assistants through a reading of the issues, as no index to Muncie presently exists. Also included are the numerous wire service stories, frequently testing the current opinion of Muncie residents on a variety of subjects of national interest.

Primarily for the sake of brevity, annotations are written in journalistic style or note form. They summarize the content of the reference and, when apparent, indicate the author's viewpoint. Cross-references to related works are indicated by the notation 'see item ___.'

Databases and indexes searched for this bibliography include
Social Science Citations Index, Sociological Abstracts, BRS,
Dissertation Abstracts International and Readers Guide.   The
Middletown III Project also has supplied lists of publications.
In addition, we have examined the holdings of the Middletown
Studies Collections, located in Ball State University Libraries
Special Collections.

The Middletown Studies Collections contain archival as well as
printed materials.   Included in the holdings are Middletown III,
Black Middletown and Middletown Film Project collections.   Other
archival collections of Middletown materials are held by the
Library of Congress, Sarah Lawrence College, Columbia University
Oral History Collection, Time Inc. Archives, North Texas State
University Libraries, and the Rockefeller Archive Center.

INTRODUCTION

When Robert S. and Helen M. Lynd stepped off the train in Muncie, Indiana, in January, 1923, little did they know that they were to initiate a chain of events which continues to this day. They were about to begin a study of the community which was a pioneering effort using the same participant observation techniques anthropologists had used to study exotic societies in remote corners of the world. Their research culminated in a book, MIDDLETOWN (1929).

MIDDLETOWN was an immediate success. It received a front page review in the NEW YORK TIMES in which Stuart Chase prophetically proclaimed, "This book should be inscribed on tablets of stone and preserved for future generations." The book has remained in print ever since and is so highly regarded that Robert B. Downs included it as one of the twenty-five books THAT CHANGED AMERICA (1970). It has proven to be a vast resource for anthropologists, sociologists, historians, and others interested in American society and culture ever since.

Robert Lynd returned to Muncie in 1935 to determine the impact of the Great Depression upon the community. The second trip produced MIDDLETOWN IN TRANSITION (1937) which emphasized the exercise of power in Muncie by the "X" family and the persistence of older values in a town relying heavily upon federal relief funds. The second book in the series was not as popular as the first, but it, too, has become part of the canon of community studies.

The interest in community studies, however, waned among sociologists in the post-World War II era and the Middletown books were relegated to a position of historical classics, read but not emulated. The situation changed in 1975 when Theodore Caplow, a professor of sociology at the University of Virginia and a former student of Robert Lynd, along with two colleagues from Brigham Young University, Howard M. Bahr and Bruce A. Chadwick, determined to replicate the work of the Lynds and returned to Muncie.

The team spent more time in Muncie than had the Lynds; they
employed a larger number of assistants; and, of course, they had,
and used, sophisticated computers to process data. The scholars'
effort resulted in a flood of articles, which still continues,
and two books, MIDDLETOWN FAMILIES (1982) and ALL FAITHFUL PEOPLE
(1983). These works, although not yet challenging the Lynds' in
importance, have nonetheless had considerable impact upon
scholars and the general public. As the work of Middletown III
continues, one may expect that the impact will increase.

At exactly the same time that MIDDLETOWN FAMILIES was published a
media event also appeared on national public television which
probably made Middletown more familiar and famous than any of the
articles or books written about the town. It was the Middletown
Film Series, which was composed of six films on life in Muncie
made by Peter Davis. The series became controversial when one
segment, "17" was written by the producer after a dispute with
the head of PBS. The withdrawal stimulated interest; and when
the film was finally shown in theaters, it further publicized the
community. The dispute and the critical reaction to the films
and to the withdrawal of the films also generated many newspaper
and magazine articles, both from those interested in films and
from those interested in community studies.

Finally, during the '80s, the Center for Middletown Studies was
established. The Center has several goals, among them to
encourage research on Muncie and to promote the name of the
center. The Center, as part of its mission, collects materials,
both historical and contemporary, pertaining to Middletown. It
has sponsored this book whose purpose is to aid and further
scholarship on Muncie and the efforts to understand the
community. Those connected with the Center as research
associates or fellows have also expanded the list of available
materials on the community.

All of this activity has occurred at a time when community
studies has once again attracted more favor and interest in the
scholarly community. Particularly in Great Britain, sociologists
are returning both to the idea of doing community studies and to
the method of participant observation. The realization that
national statistics tend to smooth over regional and local
variations, especially at times when certain areas are enjoying
much prosperity while others are depressed, has in part,
contributed to the revival.

This annotated bibliography is offered in the hopes that it, too,
will add to the growth of community studies in general and
Middletown in particular.

Dwight W. Hoover

ACKNOWLEDGMENTS

The authors wish to thank the following for their generous advice and encouragement: the Center for Middletown Studies Advisory Committee, Muncie Newspapers Executive Editor, Bill Spurgeon, Ball State University Provost, Warren Vander Hill, and Middletown III directors Theodore Caplow, Howard Bahr and Bruce Chadwick. We also are most grateful to the BSU Honors College for awarding an Undergraduate Fellows grant, which funded the research assistance of Cathy Penas. In addition, we express our appreciation to Dean Michael Wood for providing time for library personnel to pursue this project.

Furthermore, we wish to acknowledge our gratitude to Ball State University interlibrary loan librarian Veva McCoskey and her staff for locating copies of numerous citations, and to reference librarian Neal Coil for providing bibliographic and editorial expertise. The reference staff of Muncie Public Library also aided us in identifying several particulary obscure sources. Several individuals in BSU Libraries Special Collections spent long hours searching and verifying citations for this bibliography. They include University Archivist Nancy Turner and research assistants Jayme Moore, Marjorie Akin, Deborah Eckstein, Mary Martin, Bruce Bohlander and Terri Robar. Center for Middletown Studies assistant Jody Judd also helped with wordprocessing. More than anyone else, however, Special Collections library technician Mary Lou Gentis deserves a special thank you for researching, editing, and preparing the many drafts of the manuscript.

David C. Tambo
Dwight W. Hoover
John D. Hewitt

October 1987

Middletown

1924

1. "Nearly Everybody Now Has Car Here: Robert Lynde [sic] Gives Interesting Figures about Muncie in Talk to Kiwanians." MUNCIE EVENING PRESS, 29 October 1924, p. 2.

   Notes that Robert Lynd is in Muncie to do social survey and is sharing some preliminary findings, particularly in regard to changes in use of leisure time between 1890 and present day.

2. "Kiwanians Hear Reports on City: Social Research Worker Addresses Regular Meeting of Local Club." MUNCIE MORNING STAR, 30 October 1924, p. 14.

   Describes Robert Lynd's talk on changes in Muncie, as shown by analysis of newspaper files from January 1890 and January 1924. Notes increase in leisure activities, including participation in Muncie's 500 clubs.

3. "Lynde [sic] Discusses Muncie Affairs." MUNCIE EVENING PRESS, 4 November 1924, p. 2.

   Brief note of talk to Rotarians about research findings on civic groups and local public library.

1928

4. Benchley, Robert. "The Typical New Yorker." YALE REVIEW 18 (September 1928): 39-47.

   Argues, in apparent reference to forthcoming MIDDLETOWN, that the New Yorker is more of a "real American" than Muncie resident.

1928

5.   Seldes, Gilbert. "The Road to Athens." BOOKMAN
     68 (October 1928): 224-27.

     States that emerging sociological interest is
     symptomatic of a more introspective America.
     Comparison of MAIN STREET, LIVING IN THE TWENTIETH
     CENTURY, and CIVILIZATION with MIDDLETOWN. Finds
     MIDDLETOWN more realistic.

1929

6.   Lynd, Robert S., and Helen M. Lynd. MIDDLETOWN:
     A STUDY IN CONTEMPORARY AMERICAN CULTURE. New York:
     Harcourt, Brace and Company, 1929.

     Initial study, based on 1924-25 research, uses
     social anthropological approach to examine six areas
     of activity in Muncie, Indiana: getting a living,
     making a home, training the young, using leisure,
     engaging in religious practice and engaging in
     community activities.

7.   Mull, June. "Book Reveals Cross-Section of
     Muncie's Community Life." MUNCIE MORNING
     STAR, 11 January 1929, p. 3.

     Notes that Muncie residents' curiosity about
     MIDDLETOWN now satisfied with arrival of copies at
     public library and local bookstores. Identity of
     Middletown, although not revealed in book, is
     recognized from aerial photograph of Muncie on dust
     jacket.

8.   Duffus, R.L. "Getting at the Truth About an Average
     American Town." NEW YORK TIMES BOOK REVIEW, 20
     January 1929, p. 3.

     Review of MIDDLETOWN, noting unflattering nature of
     Lynds' portrayal. Discusses control of community by
     business elite, pressures on residents to conform to
     community standards, and general preoccupation with
     money.

1929

9.   Review of MIDDLETOWN. OUTLOOK AND INDEPENDENT
      151 (23 January 1929): 158.

      Short note, finding study to be provocative and
      valuable.

10.   Review of MIDDLETOWN. BOSTON EVENING TRANSCRIPT,
      30 January 1929, sec. 3, p. 2.

      Summarizes Lynds' conclusions, noting usefulness to
      municipal officials and others interested in
      promoting "civic progress."

11.   Review of MIDDLETOWN. WISCONSIN LIBRARY BULLETIN 25
      (February 1929): 73.

      Short notice of publication.

12.   Shaw, W.B. Review of MIDDLETOWN. REVIEW OF
      REVIEWS 79 (February 1929): 28, 30.

      Finds study very readable and worthwhile, largely
      because it raises more questions than it answers.
      Ventures guess, based on internal evidence, that
      Middletown is in southern Ohio or Indiana.

13.   Chase, Stuart. "The Bewildered Western World."
      BOOKS (New York Herald Tribune), 3 February 1929,
      pp. 1-2.

      Review of MIDDLETOWN, noting its ethnographic
      perspective and findings reminiscent of Sinclair
      Lewis' BABBITT. Sees Middletown residents of 1920s
      less in control of their individual destinies than
      their late nineteenth century counterparts, and
      hence more bewildered by what is going on around
      them.

1929

14.   Chase, Stuart.   "Life in Middletown."   NATION
      128 (6 February 1929): 164.

      Review of MIDDLETOWN, emphasizing leisure
      activities.

15.   Nevins, Allan.   "Fascinating Spectacle of an
      American Town Under the Microscope."   NEW YORK
      WORLD, 17 February 1929, sec. M, p. 10.

      Review of MIDDLETOWN, arguing that most educated
      Americans already have mental picture of the
      ordinary small American city but actually it is "a
      stereotype of certain surface aspects of such
      centres, and nothing more."   Finds study
      enlightening in its myriad of details, from
      automobiles to community's relative cultural
      poverty.

16.   Garrison, Winfred Ernest.   "An American Cross-
      Section."   CHRISTIAN CENTURY 46 (21 February
      1929): 265.

      Review of MIDDLETOWN, focusing on religious aspects
      of the study.   Agrees with Lynds' reticence to use
      the term "typical," although does seem broadly
      representative of many communities.

17.   Grattan, C.H.   "A Typical American City."   NEW
      REPUBLIC 58 (27 February 1929): 48-49.

      Discusses changes in Middletown regarding home,
      leisure, and industry.

18.   "An American Town."   TIMES LITERARY SUPPLEMENT
      (London), 28 February 1929, p. 155.

      Review of MIDDLETOWN, applauding Lynds' use of
      anthropological techniques to investigate American,
      rather than a remote, people.   Notes rapid change in
      Middletown since 1890 and wonders if residents of an
      English town would have been as receptive to such an
      inquiry.

1929

19.   Brickell, Herschel. "An American Small Town."
       NORTH AMERICAN REVIEW 227 (March 1929): adv.

       Short review of MIDDLETOWN, calling the community
       "typical" and illustrative of "cross-section of our
       culture."

20.   Mencken, H.L. "A City in Moronia." AMERICAN
       MERCURY 16 (March 1929): 379-81.

       Argues that Middletown study gives excellent
       description of the typical American with his
       "unbelievable stupidities."

21.   Review of MIDDLETOWN. BOOKLIST 25 (March
       1929): 244.

       Short notice, viewing Middletown as "representative
       small American city."

22.   Busch, Henry M. "Main Street Under a Microscope."
       SURVEY 61 (15 March 1929): 775-77.

       Review of MIDDLETOWN, drawing attention to
       its analysis of business/working class mentalities.

23.   Williams, Whiting. "Through the Looking Glass."
       SATURDAY REVIEW OF LITERATURE 5 (30 March
       1929): 824.

       Review of MIDDLETOWN, finding its portrayal
       fascinating yet disturbing. Criticizes "method of
       presentation" and authors' opposition to laissez-
       faire economics.

24.   Review of MIDDLETOWN. AMERICAN HISTORICAL REVIEW 34
       (April 1929): 695.

       Short, favorable note questioning, however, extent
       to which generalizations can be made from limited
       number of examples.

1929

25.   Dewey, John. "The House Divided against Itself."
       NEW REPUBLIC 58 (24 April 1929): 270-71.

       Argues against economic determinism of a "money
       culture," as depicted in MIDDLETOWN. Suggests that
       industrialization has wrought great changes, tying
       worker to machine, but this need not be so.
       American society can harness industrialization but
       must question ideals which glorify quest for
       monetary gain.

26.   Zorbaugh, Harvey W. Review of MIDDLETOWN. JOURNAL OF
       EDUCATIONAL SOCIOLOGY 2 (May 1929): 549.

       Praises study, noting it fills gap in literature of
       the community, which has focused on rural and large
       city entities.

27.   Ward, Harry F. "Seeing Ourselves." WORLD TOMORROW 12
       (May 1929): 234.

       Review of MIDDLETOWN, arguing that despite Lynds'
       caution against viewing community as typical, "our
       life is sufficiently standardized that the peculiar
       characteristics of any town do not significantly
       alter the general pattern of existence."

28.   "Discusses Book About Muncie." MUNCIE EVENING
       PRESS, 7 May 1929, p. 5.

       Review of MIDDLETOWN by Dean Ralph Noyer of
       Ball State Teachers College for Muncie Rotarians.
       Suggests Lynds brought biases with them, including
       viewpoint that Muncie was preoccupied with "dollar-
       chasing."

29.   "Reviews and Notices: Middletown." INDIANA
       MAGAZINE OF HISTORY 25 (June 1929): 178-79.

       Quotes Stuart Chase (item 14) and John Dewey (item
       25) on scholarly importance of Lynds' study.

1929

30.   Ware, Norman J. Review of MIDDLETOWN. AMERICAN
       ECONOMIC REVIEW 19 (June 1929): 328-29.

       Reflects upon contribution of Lynds' "actual
       observation" approach to community studies, as well
       as "cultural lag" evident in Middletown lives, and
       unnamed research site, guessing it to be Indiana.

31.   "On Herd Life." NEW YORK TIMES, 23 June 1929,
       sec. 3, p. 4.

       Discusses Fosdick's speech at Smith College (see
       item 32), arguing that individuality does exist in
       smaller communities, dullness of life to some extent
       may be in the eye of the researcher, and even
       "despised 'herd' has its dreams."

32.   Fosdick, Raymond B. "The Adventurous Life." NEW
       YORK TIMES, 23 June 1929, sec. 9, pp. 1, 6.

       Address to graduating class at Smith College,
       stressing need for independence and individuality in
       a life of change, rather than uniformity of
       Middletown lives.

33.   "Contemporary America." SPECTATOR 142 (29 June
       1929): 1016.

       Review of MIDDLETOWN, focusing on Lynds' treatment
       of leisure and education.

34.   Review of MIDDLETOWN. CATHOLIC WORLD 129 (August 1929):
       634-35.

       Reports findings in MIDDLETOWN about material
       progress in recent years, but also abundant evidence
       of moral and spiritual decline.

1929

35.   Mortimer, Raymond. "A Tribe in the Middle West."
        NATION AND ATHENAEUM 45 (10 August 1929): 627-28.

        Review of MIDDLETOWN, comparing its findings to
        English society of 1920s.

36.   Steiner, J. F. Review of MIDDLETOWN. SOCIAL
        SERVICE REVIEW 3 (September 1929): 506-9.

        Questions anonymity of Middletown, delayed
        publication and lack of reference to Negroes, but
        sees study as useful for social planners.

37.   "Muncie Again Is Lynd's Subject." MUNCIE EVENING
        PRESS, 24 October 1929, p. 2.

        Excerpts from Robert Lynd's contribution to
        symposium entitled "What Is Right With America?" In
        November issue of MCCALL'S MAGAZINE (see item 38).

38.   Forman, Henry James. "What is Right with America?"
        MCCALL'S, November 1929.

        Uses quotations from Sinclair Lewis, Walter
        Lippmann, Will Durant and Robert Lynd to support the
        premise that America is moving "toward a great
        culture" and not "drifting backward." Lynd contends
        there are new social problems arising due to
        traditional values.

39.   Forman, Henry James. "What's Right with America?"
        REVIEW OF REVIEWS AND WORLD'S WORK (November 1929):
        89-90.

        Includes interviews with Sinclair Lewis, Walter
        Lippmann, Robert S. Lynd, and Will Durant.
        Excerpted from November 1929 issue of MCCALL'S
        MAGAZINE.

1929

40.   Hunt, Douglas L. Review of MIDDLETOWN. ANNALS OF THE
       AMERICAN ACADEMY OF POLITICAL AND SOCIAL SCIENCE 146
       (November 1929): 271-72.

       Finds depiction of Middletown life unsettling,
       showing changes largely in material culture rather
       than attitudes. Draws attention to appendix
       entitled "Notes on Method."

41.   "Muncie Schools Ready to Receive Criticisms."
       MUNCIE EVENING PRESS, 1 November 1929, p. 13.

       Glen D. Brown, business and vocational director of
       Muncie City Schools, notes attempt to persuade Lynds
       to change "Training the Young" section of MIDDLETOWN
       because of changes recently made in the school
       corporation, including administrative
       reorganization, new programs and added research.

42.   Review of MIDDLETOWN. OPEN SHELF (Cleveland Public
       Library), December 1929, p. 152.

       Brief notice, labelling Middletown a "sample
       American community."

1930

43.   Lynd, Robert S., and Helen M. Lynd. MEDICAL CARE IN
       MIDDLETOWN. Washington D.C.: Committee on the Costs
       of Medical Care, 1930.

       Excerpted from chapter 25 of MIDDLETOWN (see
       item 6).

1930

44.   "Muncie Not as Book Suggests." MUNCIE EVENING PRESS, 26
        March 1930, p. 16.

        Reports opinion of Lloyd Sweeting, statistician and
        researcher for national advertisers, that Lynds' use
        of figures from relatively few sources does not tell
        whole Muncie story. Describes test-marketing
        techniques and notes that cities like Muncie,
        "undoubtedly the fundamental heart of America," are
        obvious areas for further market research.

45.   Douglas, W.A.S. "The Mayor of Middletown." AMERICAN
        MERCURY 20 (August 1930): 478-86.

        Account of George Dale's struggle as newspaperman
        against Ku Klux Klan and his rise to mayor during
        time of first Middletown study. Includes discussion
        of political corruption in Middletown.

46.   White, E.C. "Is Muncie Really Middletown?" MUNCIE
        EVENING PRESS, 10 October 1930, p. 20.

        Muncie woman argues that Lynds arrived with
        preconceptions, creating a self-fulfilling prophecy.

1931

47.   Chase, Stuart. MEXICO: A STUDY OF TWO AMERICAS. New
        York: Literary Guild, 1931.

        Draws numerous comparisons between Tepotztlan and
        Middletown arguing that former, with 99% Indian
        population, is more "American" although in different
        sense.

1931

48.   Lynd, Robert, and Helen Lynd. MIDDLETOWN: ETHNOGRAPHIE
        DE L'AMERICAIN MOYEN. Paris: editions du Carrefour,
        1931.

        French translation of item 6, with new preface and
        glossary of American terms.

49.   Roll, Charles. INDIANA, ONE HUNDRED AND FIFTY
        YEARS OF AMERICAN DEVELOPMENT. Chicago: Lewis,
        1931: V. pp. 191-192.

        Biographical entry on George Dale, noting fight with
        Klan and referring to fact he was mayor of city
        widely renowned as Middletown.

50.   "Muncie Plan Adopted as U.S. Model." MUNCIE
        EVENING PRESS, 20 February 1931, p. 1.

        Muncie's Community Garden Association idea, which
        provides means for unemployed to raise gardens at
        home, to be used elsewhere in Indiana and possibly
        other states.

51.   Potter, Paul. "Gardens Solve Food Problem for
        the Needy: Muncie Plan Hailed Boon to Hoosierland."
        CHICAGO TRIBUNE, 21 August 1931, sec. 1, p. 17.

        Discusses use of vacant property for gardens to help
        feed needy, along with increasing employment,
        resulting in less money spent by taxpayers.

52.   Lockwood, George B. "Something Good Out of
        Middletown." MUNCIE EVENING PRESS, 26 August
        1931, p. 4.

        Draws attention to Rockefeller Foundation's interest
        in Muncie, first with Lynd study and more recently
        in regard to community garden plan. Suggests that
        data in MIDDLETOWN may have been accurate but made
        to fit social and economic preconceptions.

1931

53.   Review of MIDDLETOWN. MICHIGAN HISTORY MAGAZINE
        15 (Winter 1931): 157-58.

        Finds literary quality and scholarship excellent,
        and picture of Muncie presented accurately.

54.   "National Magazine Describes Results of 'Muncie
        Plan.'" MUNCIE EVENING PRESS, 11 December 1931,
        pp. 10-11.

        Reports national attention to local jobs plan.
        Article to appear in LADIES HOME JOURNAL (see item
        55). Reprint of article follows.

1932

55.   Hawkins, James H. "Jobs for the Jobless: How
        the Muncie Plan Creates Employment." LADIES HOME
        JOURNAL 49 (January 1932): 22, 39.

        Describes Chamber of Commerce efforts to create
        construction jobs through house modernization
        campaign. Implies that if plan works in "average
        American city" like Muncie, it will work elsewhere.

56.   Cable, J. Ray. Review of MIDDLETOWN. SOCIAL
        SCIENCE 7 (April 1932): 198-99.

        Describes work as an adventure in observation or
        laboratory study in search of a thesis.

57.   "Dean Noyer Gives an Interpretation of 'Middletown' in
        Club Address." MUNCIE MORNING STAR, 27 September
        1932, sec. 1 p. 12.

        Short notice on Dean Ralph Noyer's talk to the
        Muncie Women's Club, noting criticism surrounding
        Middletown study waning.

1934

58. "Middletown -- Ten Years After. Pt. I: How
     'Middletown' Came Through." BUSINESS WEEK, 26 May
     1934, pp. 15, 16.

     Reports findings of 1934 survey on living, working
     and buying habits of Middletown. Notes increase in
     absentee ownership of factories and down-turn of
     auto industry, but healthy sales of canning jars and
     beer bottles, and Ball family support of Muncie
     banks, helping stave off worst effects of
     Depression.

59. "Middletown -- Ten Years After. Pt. II: How
     'Middletown' Buys." BUSINESS WEEK, 2 June 1934,
     pp. 18, 20.

     Reports some upturn in spending, more among farmers
     than laborers. Notes, however, that some Muncie
     businesses hurt by Indianapolis competition,
     resulting from improved transportation links.

60. "Middletown -- Ten Years After. Pt. III: 'Middletown'
     at Work - and Out of Work." BUSINESS WEEK, 9 June
     1934, pp. 12, 14.

     Focuses on labor situation, including high
     unemployment among migrants from Tennessee and
     Kentucky who had moved north during better times.
     Also discusses local relief efforts such as
     subsistence gardens, upswing of auto industry, and
     increase in labor union membership.

1935

61. "Lynd, Author of Middletown Back in City after 10
     Years." MUNCIE EVENING PRESS, 12 June 1935, p. 1.

     Provides update on Lynds and coworkers, noting that
     current research on changes of last decade may
     result in appendix to MIDDLETOWN but certainly not
     another book.

1935

62.   "Check Changes in 'Middletown.'" MUNCIE MORNING
       STAR, 13 June 1935, p. 6.

       Note on Robert Lynd's arrival in Muncie ten years
       after the original study to check changes which may
       have occurred. Speculates whether or not he may
       publish appendix to next edition of MIDDLETOWN.

63.   Dale, George R. "The Editor's Corner." POST-DEMOCRAT
       (Muncie), 14 June 1935, p. 4.

       Former Muncie mayor, profiled in MIDDLETOWN, notes
       return of Lynd, "who carved our vitals ten years
       ago," and offers pointed comments on Muncie's mixed
       reaction to his work.

64.   "Middletown Author to Address Rotary." MUNCIE
       EVENING PRESS, 17 June 1935, p. 5.

       Brief note that Lynd and research staff of five in
       Muncie and will speak to group 18 June 1935.

65.   Dale, George R. "The Editor's Corner." POST-DEMOCRAT
       (Muncie), 21 June 1935, p. 4.

       Argues that Lynd's few days of research in Muncie to
       research changes of last decade are insufficient to
       produce sequel to MIDDLETOWN.

1935

66.   Kelso, Paul. "'Middletown' Authors Leaving Today After
       Two Weeks' Visit." MUNCIE MORNING STAR, 26 June
       1935, pp. 1, 11.

       Muncie gives collective sigh of relief upon Lynd's
       departure after two weeks of intense fact-finding
       and interviewing. States that he will examine new
       data before deciding whether to publish as appendix
       to next edition of MIDDLETOWN.

1937

67. Lynd, Robert S., and Helen M. Lynd. MIDDLETOWN
     IN TRANSITION: A STUDY IN CULTURAL CONFLICTS. New
     York: Harcourt, Brace and Company, 1937.

     Restudy, based on 1935 research, uses same general
     approach as MIDDLETOWN (see item 6) but greater
     emphasis on role of "X" (Ball) family in local power
     structure. Analyzes impact of Depression on
     community institutions.

68. Melcher, Frederic G. "Gardening in Middletown."
     PUBLISHERS' WEEKLY 131, 7 (13 February 1937): 807.

     Editorial reflecting upon role of gardening in
     Muncie society, as described in advance proofs of
     MIDDLETOWN IN TRANSITION.

69. Lewellen, John. "Country's Ace Photographer to
     Take Picture Series Here." MUNCIE EVENING PRESS, 5
     April 1937, p. 2.

     Notes Margaret Bourke-White's arrival to photograph
     Muncie scenes for LIFE MAGAZINE. Includes
     biographical sketch.

70. "Famous Photographer Poses With City Officials." MUNCIE
     EVENING PRESS, 6 April 1937, p. 1.

     Account of Bourke-White photographing city council
     session. Includes photograph of her with council
     members.

71. Kelso, Paul. "City Council Goes on Parade before
     Famed Camera Artist." MUNCIE MORNING STAR, 6 April
     1937, pp. 1, 3.

     Describes Bourke-White's photographing of city
     council session, and provides background on her
     career.

1937

72.   "Rotarians Face the Camera." MUNCIE EVENING
       PRESS, 6 April 1937, p. 2.

       Notes appearance of Bourke-White who "had the
       Rotarian membership applauding the speaker in slow
       motion, so the action wouldn't blur the picture."

73.   "Muncie Is Honored." MUNCIE MORNING STAR, 7
       April 1937, p. 16.

       Short notice of Bourke-White's arrival, claiming
       Muncie appreciates its national status as "the
       typical American city."

74.   Lynd, Robert S., and Helen Merrell Lynd. "Reading
           During the Depression." PUBLISHERS' WEEKLY 131 (10
           April 1937): 1587-90.

       Slightly condensed section from "Spending Leisure"
       chapter of MIDDLETOWN IN TRANSITION. Notes book to
       be released 22 April 1937.

75.   Lewellen, John. "Leisure-Time Increase in Muncie
           Observed by Lynd." MUNCIE EVENING PRESS, 12 April
           1937, p. 3.

       Notes April 22 publication date for Lynds' second
       study and describes section on Muncie reading
       habits, appearing in PUBLISHERS' WEEKLY.

76.   "Famed Photographer Tells of Experiences."
       MUNCIE MORNING STAR, 13 April 1937, p. 9.

       Short notice of Bourke-White's talk at Muncie Camera
       Club meeting.

1937

77. "Muncie Unlikely to Agree With Findings Of Dr.
     Lynd." MUNCIE EVENING PRESS, 13 April 1937, p. 2.

     Review of forthcoming book, MIDDLETOWN IN
     TRANSITION, predicting adverse local criticism to
     Lynd conclusions such as statement "'Middletown' is
     likely to continue its course of reluctant
     adaptation and expediency into the future."

78. "Photographer Club's Speaker." MUNCIE MORNING
     STAR, 13 April 1937, p. 9.

     Account of Bourke-White's talk to Muncie Business
     and Professional Women's Club.

79. "Takes Own Medicine! Margaret Bourke-White
     Faces Dozens of Amateur Cameramen and Smiles Through
     It All." MUNCIE EVENING PRESS, 13 April 1937, p.
     16.

     Describes Muncie Camera Club members photographing
     Bourke-White during speech to the group. Also
     refers to exhibit of her prints at meeting.

80. Sutton, Wilbur E. "We Peer into a Cracked
     Mirror." MUNCIE EVENING PRESS, 16 April 1937, pp.
     1, 6.

     Review of MIDDLETOWN IN TRANSITION, suggesting that
     in parts Lynd "has been made the victim of certain
     community gossips." Cites incident of local
     columnist supposedly hauled before bankers after
     writing critical article and notes this never
     happened.

81. "Famous Photographer Ends Camera Study of Muncie."
     MUNCIE EVENING PRESS, 20 April 1937, p. 4.

     Bourke-White leaving after stay of more than two
     weeks. Tells of hundreds of negatives sent to New
     York to be developed.

1937

82.   Aikman, Duncan. "Mr. Babbitt Still Runs Middletown."
      SATURDAY REVIEW OF LITERATURE 15 (24 April 1937):
      3-4, 14.

      Stresses thoroughness of second Lynd study, as
      contrasted with more informal methods of "amateur
      sociologists." Notes that Middletown still retains
      conservative mindset depicted in initial 1924-25
      study.

83.   Herskovits, Melville J. "American Microcosm."
      NATION 144 (24 April 1937): 474, 476.

      Review of MIDDLETOWN IN TRANSITION, finding it much
      more mature and sure in its presentation than
      predecessor which tended to mask its biases with a
      supposedly impartial, thesis-like approach.

84.   "Middletown: Typical American City Has Changed Little in
      a Decade." LITERARY DIGEST 123 (24 April 1937):
      32-33.

      Review of MIDDLETOWN IN TRANSITION, reporting Lynds'
      findings and quoting then-mayor Rollin H. Bunch
      saying Muncie enjoys its typicality.

85.   Richards, Gertrude R.B. "Middletown is now in
      Transition." BOSTON EVENING TRANSCRIPT, 24 April
      1937, sec. 6, p. 2.

      Review of MIDDLETOWN IN TRANSITION, focusing on
      Muncie's conservatism, lack of faith in federal
      programs, and inability to learn any lessons from
      Depression.

86.   "Seems to be the Same Old Middletown." BUSINESS WEEK,
      24 April 1937, pp. 46, 47.

      Review of MIDDLETOWN IN TRANSITION, focusing on
      effects of Depression on local business climate.

1937

87.   Chase, Stuart. "Middletown, as American as a Baked
       Apple: Superb Study of a Corn-Belt City in Boom and
       Depression." BOOKS (NEW YORK HERALD TRIBUNE), 25
       April 1937, pp. 1-2.

       Review of MIDDLETOWN IN TRANSITION, finding it
       better than MIDDLETOWN (favorably reviewed in 1929,
       especially in terms of discussion of social change).
       Notes with some surprise that traditional values
       remain in MIDDLETOWN, despite Depression. No
       longer, however, are they accepted uncritically.

88.   Duffus, R.L. "Middletown Ten Years After: The Lynd's
       Continue Their Study of a Typical American
       Community." NEW YORK TIMES BOOK REVIEW, 25 April
       1937, pp. 1, 16.

       Review of MIDDLETOWN IN TRANSITION, focusing on
       treatment of employer/employee relationships and
       finding new study even more important than its
       predecessor.

89.   Kelso, Paul. "Middletown in Transition: The Lynds Offer
       an Essentially Faithful Word Picture Not Only of
       Muncie, but of All America, Listing Our Virtues and
       Faults." MUNCIE SUNDAY STAR, 25 April 1937, sec. 2,
       pp. 1, 9.

       Describes business class characteristics and control
       over many facets of city life. Also discusses
       politics, labor, Ball family, and club life, with
       frequent quotes from MIDDLETOWN IN TRANSITION.

90.   Straton, Hillyer H. "Ex-New Yorker on 'Middletown.'"
       MUNCIE EVENING PRESS, 29 April 1937, p. 4.

       First Baptist Church pastor, previously from New
       York, takes issue with "attitude of superiority
       assumed by the Lynds" and finds many admirable
       things in Muncie.

1937

91.   Brickell, Herschel. "The Literary Landscape" REVIEW OF
       REVIEWS 95 (May 1937): 58.

       Review of MIDDLETOWN IN TRANSITION, noting lack of
       attitudinal change among Middletown residents,
       despite Depression.

92.   Review of MIDDLETOWN IN TRANSITION. BOOKLIST 33 (May
       1937): 260.

       Short notice, describing ways latest study updates
       earlier MIDDLETOWN.

93.   Review of MIDDLETOWN IN TRANSITION. WISCONSIN LIBRARY
       BULLETIN 88 (May 1937): 98.

       Short notice of publication.

94.   "Mirror of America." CHRISTIAN CENTURY 54 (5 May
       1937): 574-76.

       Review of MIDDLETOWN IN TRANSITION, noting community
       adherence to laissez-faire ideals and relative lack
       of religious change. Finds that Middletown has not
       learned much from events of last decade.

95.   Schmiedeler, Edgar. "If Rip Van Winkle Awoke."
       COMMONWEAL 26 (7 May 1937): 51-52.

       Review of MIDDLETOWN IN TRANSITION, emphasizing
       relative lack of change since initial study.

96.   Bourke-White, Margaret. "Muncie Ind. Is the Great
       'U.S. Middletown.'" LIFE, 10 May 1937, pp. 15-25.

       Photographic essay of Munsonians from all walks of
       life. Shot to coincide with publication of
       MIDDLETOWN IN TRANSITION.

1937

97. Cowley, Malcolm. "Still Middletown?" NEW REPUBLIC 91
     (12 May 1937): 23-24.

     Review of MIDDLETOWN IN TRANSITION, suggesting that
     Muncie's social values perhaps not as immutable as
     Lynds thought, one indicator being Roosevelt's 59
     per cent of city's vote in 1936 election, despite
     its traditional conservative bent.

98. "American Way of Life Viewed in Sharp Relief." CHICAGO
     DAILY TRIBUNE, 15 May 1937, p. 12.

     Review of MIDDLETOWN IN TRANSITION, finding it a
     fascinating depiction of American way of life.

99. "Catholic Priest Comments on Findings of Dr. Lynd."
     MUNCIE EVENING PRESS, 22 May 1937, p. 8.

     Notes response of Father Edgar J. Cyr, pastor of St.
     Mary's Church, to prior review of MIDDLETOWN IN
     TRANSITION appearing in May 16 issue of Catholic
     newspaper OUR SUNDAY VISITOR, in which local church
     criticized for lack of participation in politics or
     other public concerns, and small enrollment in
     parochial school.

100. Review of MIDDLETOWN IN TRANSITION. OPEN SHELF
     (Cleveland Public Library), May-June 1937, p. 9.

     Brief description, calling work "a study in cultural
     conflicts."

101. Johnson, Alvin. "Middletown Revisited." YALE REVIEW
     n.s., 26 (Summer 1937): 814-17.

     Review of MIDDLETOWN IN TRANSITION, finding restudy
     better than original. Notes that, despite
     Depression, not all that much change, only some
     weakening of old values.

1937

102.   Cousins, Norman B. Review of MIDDLETOWN IN TRANSITION.
         CURRENT HISTORY 46 (June 1937): 2-5.

         Compares Lynds' Middletown and John Dollard's less
         typical Southerntown, with an agrarian past and
         substantial black population. Notes effect of
         Depression on Middletown, resulting in "reluctant
         adaptation."

103.   Fuller, Raymond G. "Middletown Revisited." SURVEY 73
         (June 1937): 204.

         Finds MIDDLETOWN IN TRANSITION more mature and
         lively than its predecessor, but is discouraged that
         conservative, nondissenting, Babbitt-like Middletown
         seems to have learned nothing from Depression.

104.   Sears, William P., Jr. Review of MIDDLETOWN IN
         TRANSITION. EDUCATION 57 (June 1937): 646.

         Notes that Middletown researchers expected to find
         major changes, due to tumultuous events of last
         decade, but instead discovered a basic continuity of
         attitudes, with some less-dramatic variations.

105.   Chamberlain, John. "Books." SCRIBNER'S MAGAZINE 102
         (July 1937): 62-66.

         Review of MIDDLETOWN IN TRANSITION, noting reluctant
         community change in last decade and continued
         "omnipresent and pervasive averageness." Criticizes
         Muncie for anti-union attitudes, "Big Ownership" of
         means of production, dislike of radicals/-
         foreigners/Negroes/Jews, and religion's lack of
         social conscience.

106.   "More Comment on 'Middletown': Lynds' Book Reviewed in
         Scribner's Magazine." MUNCIE MORNING STAR, 24 June
         1937, p. 14.

         Response to Chamberlain's review (see item 105).
         Raises question whether Middletown is really a
         "typical" city.

1937

107.   "Large-scale Drama."   CHRISTIAN SCIENCE MONITOR,
         1 July 1937, p. 18.

         Review of MIDDLETOWN IN TRANSITION, finding it a
         shrewd analysis but arguing its mid-Depression
         pessimism is outdated and authors' preconceptions
         cause distortions, particularly in overemphasis of
         class feeling.

108.   Lewellen, John.   "Typical Muncie's Typical Family."
         LIFE 5 July 1937, p. 74.

         Letter to editor, citing local adverse criticism to
         social extremes portrayed in Bourke-White photo-
         essay (see item 96).   Presents, instead, short
         photo-essay of more "typical" Glen Craig family.

109.   Straton, Hillyer H.   "Pastor's Picture."   TIME,
         5 July 1937, p. 5.

         Letter to editor, pointing out Ball family's
         philanthropic activities and suggesting MIDDLETOWN
         IN TRANSITION tells readers more about Robert Lynd
         than Muncie.

110.   LIVING ON "MCCALL STREET" IN "MIDDLETOWN."
         [New York: McCall Corporation, August, 1937].

         Marketing tool produced by MCCALL'S MAGAZINE to show
         how "Middletown" families use MCCALL'S ideas in
         their daily lives.   Contains many photos of
         subscribers and their homes.

111.   Marsh, Donald C.   Review of MIDDLETOWN IN TRANSITION.
         AMERICAN SOCIOLOGICAL REVIEW 2 (August 1937):
         540-42.

         Finds Middletown sticking to "middle-of-the-road"
         despite Depression.

1937

112.   Review of MIDDLETOWN IN TRANSITION. CATHOLIC
        WORLD 145 (August 1937): 627-29.

        Focuses on religious section of study, decrying
        decline of morals and lack of spiritual values among
        Middletown residents. Notes, erroneously, that
        Middletown is Decatur, Indiana.

113.   Straton, Hillyer H. "Comment." MUNCIE EVENING
        PRESS, 5 August 1937, p. 1.

        Suggests that Lynds' critical examination of Muncie
        may help build better community, particularly in
        areas like beautification, higher teachers' wages
        and street improvements.

114.   Ratcliffe, S.K. "Middletown Again." SPECTATOR
        159 (27 August 1937): 354.

        Review of MIDDLETOWN IN TRANSITION, focusing on
        influence of "X" family and sobering effects of
        Depression on Middletown economy.

115.   Jones, H.M. Review of MIDDLETOWN IN TRANSITION.
        QUARTERLY BOOKLIST (Pratt Institute, Free Library),
        Autumn 1937, p. 9.

        Brief notice of publication.

116.   Jones, Howard Mumford. "Middletown Still Runs
        Mr. Babbitt." NORTH AMERICAN REVIEW 244 (Autumn
        1937): 194-201.

        Notes growth from town to small city, with increase
        of automobiles, radios and movies, establishment of
        a college, and increased power of "X" family.
        Points out hazard of using "ideal city standard" to
        measure findings.

1937

117.   "Middletown in Transition." RECREATION 31
        (September 1937): 335-36.

        Review article, with emphasis on recreational
        changes in Middletown culture.

118.   Review of MIDDLETOWN IN TRANSITION. JOURNAL OF
        HOME ECONOMICS 29 (September 1937): 472.

        Short notice of publication.

119.   Fuller, Raymond G. "Muncie Looks at Middletown." NEW
        REPUBLIC 92 (8 September 1937): 127-28.

        Expands upon comments in A STUDY OF YOUTH NEEDS (see
        item 131), regarding local ambivalence toward Lynds
        studies.

120.   Gorer, Geoffrey. "Erewhon Revisited." NEW STATESMAN &
        NATION 14 (11 September 1937): 378-380.

        Review of MIDDLETOWN IN TRANSITION, focusing on
        impact of financial slump, and Lynds' methodological
        approach. Finds chief weakness in reliance on
        statistical data to exclusion of description of
        individuals in the culture.

121.   "Middletown Revisited." TIMES LITERARY SUPPLEMENT
        (London), 11 September 1937, p. 650.

        Review of MIDDLETOWN IN TRANSITION, suggesting that
        effects of crisis like Depression perhaps more
        appropriate topic for history than sociology. Also
        points out differences in values between researchers
        and community, particularly in regard to laissez-
        faire individualism.

1937

122.   Brooks, Lee M. "Library and Workshop: Middletown in
        Transition." SOCIAL FORCES 16 (October 1937):
        150-51.

        Sees second Middletown study as illustrative of
        national trends and opinions.

123.   Brooks, Lee M. Review of MIDDLETOWN IN TRANSITION.
        SOCIAL FORCES 16 (October 1937): 150-51.

        Sees study as part of "trend in bringing into
        contemporary focus some of the standard community
        surveys of earlier years," and indicative of
        maturization process in sociology.

124.   Odegard, Peter H. Review of MIDDLETOWN IN TRANSITION.
        AMERICAN POLITICAL SCIENCE REVIEW 31 (October 1937):
        981-83.

        Disagrees with Mencken's assessment of Middletown as
        "a city in Moronia" (see item 20). Instead, sees
        it as microcosm of American society, emerging
        scarred from Depression, with its traditional
        beliefs somewhat shaken by economic realities.

125.   "Middletown Revisited." ECONOMIST 129 (2 October
        1937): 23.

        Review of MIDDLETOWN IN TRANSITION, commenting on
        resilience of the community's institutions despite
        economic decline. Finds class divisions sharpening,
        and Lynds' general tone more skeptical.

126.   "Fame of Muncie as Ideal American City Travels to Far-
        Off Capital of Austria." MUNCIE MORNING STAR, 10
        October 1937, p. 5.

        Note that Scherbaum children of Muncie received
        request from Viennese uncle to send information and
        photos of Muncie, due to its Middletown fame.

1937

127.   Bakke, E. Wight. Review of MIDDLETOWN IN TRANSITION.
        YALE LAW JOURNAL 47 (November 1937): 152-157.

        Focuses on Lynds' findings regarding widening class
        divisions and community opposition to organized
        labor. Argues many "changes" since earlier study
        may in fact reflect a more perceptive examination of
        local situation by Lynds, rather than shift in
        Middletown attitudes.

128.   Burgess, Ernest W. Review of MIDDLETOWN IN TRANSITION.
        AMERICAN JOURNAL OF SOCIOLOGY 43 (November 1937):
        486-89.

        Considers second Middletown study important for
        documentation of urban response to Depression.

129.   Schwartz, Martin D. "Middletown's Maverick Mayor."
        HARVARD GUARDIAN 2 (November 1937): 30-36.

        Account of George R. Dale's career by Muncie
        resident. Notes Lynds' discussion of Dale in local
        government section of MIDDLETOWN.

130.   Ware, Norman J. "Social Problems and Reforms."
        AMERICAN ECONOMIC REVIEW 27 (December 1937): 842-43.

        Review of MIDDLETOWN IN TRANSITION, arguing this is
        more of an interpretive study than the original and
        that it shows no community can be typical. Instead,
        more studies of variations needed for comparative
        purposes.

1938

131.   Fuller, Raymond G. A STUDY OF YOUTH NEEDS AND
        SERVICES IN MUNCIE, INDIANA: A REPORT TO THE
        AMERICAN YOUTH COMMISSION OF THE AMERICAN COUNCIL ON
        EDUCATION. Washington, D.C.: American Youth
        Commission, 1938.

        Selects Muncie as research site, due to "guinea pig"
        status derived from Lynd Middletown studies. Notes
        backlash from studies, enhancing community's
        defensiveness.

132.   Ware, Caroline F. Review of MIDDLETOWN IN TRANSITION.
        AMERICAN HISTORICAL REVIEW 43 (January 1938):
        426-27.

        Notes contribution of study to social history,
        particularly of non-elites, and to examination of
        the problem of process of change.

133.   Willey, Malcolm M. Review of MIDDLETOWN IN TRANSITION.
        ANNALS OF THE AMERICAN ACADEMY OF POLITICAL AND
        SOCIAL SCIENCE 195 (January 1938): 238-39.

        Finds restudy stimulating and insightful, more
        readable yet less methodologically rigorous than
        original, particularly in regard to attitudinal
        analysis.

134.   Review of MIDDLETOWN IN TRANSITION. JOURNAL OF
        EDUCATIONAL SOCIOLOGY 11 (February 1938): 376.

        Finds study significant but notes that many parts
        copied verbatim from first book.

135.   Merton, Robert K. Review of MIDDLETOWN IN
        TRANSITION. RURAL SOCIOLOGY 3 (March 1938):
        110-11.

        Admires Lynds' collection of data but argues that "a
        central, sociological conceptual scheme for unifying
        the observed facts is still needed."

1938

136.   Catlin, George. Review of MIDDLETOWN IN TRANSITION.
        INTERNATIONAL AFFAIRS 17 (July 1938): 560-61.

        Compares Lynd study to British counterparts, noting
        Americans are less likely to stoically accept
        limitations of their class and strive to advance
        their standing.

1939

137.   Lynd, Robert S. KNOWLEDGE FOR WHAT? Princeton,
        N.J.: Princeton University Press, 1939.

        Includes surprisingly few references to Middletown
        work.

138.   "Straughton [sic], Andrea Central Interest in Lives of
        Lynds." MUNCIE SUNDAY STAR, 12 March 1939, sec. 2,
        p. 1.

        Story on Lynd children, with background information
        on Middletown studies. Notes that Muncie
        investigation of Lynds reflects adage "turn about is
        fair play."

1941

139.   Bowman, Heath. HOOSIER. Indianapolis: Bobbs-Merrill,
        1941.

        Chapter entitled "Hoosiers in Transition" includes
        account by author, a Muncie native, of 1937 visit to
        Middletown. Local residents more upset by Bourke-
        White photo-essay in LIFE than latest Lynd study.

1941

140. "MIDDLETOWN" GOES TO SCHOOL. Chicago: Nation's
      Schools, [1941].

      Produced as a marketing tool to promote booklet
      entitled "School Market Data." Describes with
      frequent statistical data, how "typical" school
      system like Muncie educates its young.

1942

141. Sutton, Wilbur E. "Muncie Always Marches."
      In INDIANA TODAY: A WORK FOR NEWSPAPER AND
      LIBRARY REFERENCE, edited by C. Walter McCarty
      and others, 46-49. Indianapolis: Indiana Editors
      Association, 1942.

      Provides community profile, noting Muncie attempts
      to capitalize on "dubious" reputation as Middletown.

1943

142. Selby, John. "Middletown, America - 1943."
      MUNCIE MORNING STAR, 24 February 1943, p. 5.

      AP story on impact of war in Muncie, visiting
      local hotel, church and theatre, and noting first
      impression that life continues on pretty much as
      normal.

143. Selby, John. "Middletown - 1943. Sailor on a
      Street Corner." MUNCIE MORNING STAR, 25 February
      1943, p. 4.

      AP story, second in series, reporting lack of change
      in racial composition of factory workers, little
      evidence of housing shortage and good response to
      payroll savings plan and other conservation
      programs.

1944

144.   Miltenberger, Mark D., comp. MUNCIE: THE TYPICAL CITY.
        PLANNING FOR POST-WAR AND THE FUTURE OF MUNCIE.
        Muncie, Ind.: Muncie-Delaware County Post-War
        Planning Commission, 1944.

        Report on Muncie infrastructure and possible areas
        of development, capitalizing on Middletown fame
        through frequent use of slogan "The Ideal City."

145.   Martin, John Bartlow. "Is Muncie Still Middletown?"
        HARPER'S MAGAZINE 189 (July 1944): 97-109.

        Indianapolis reporter visiting wartime Muncie finds
        desire to end war but fear of future, strong
        isolationist tendencies, and day-to-day concerns
        focusing mostly on making a living.

146.   Clark, Mary Alice. "Muncie Is Still Middletown,
        if Article True, Says Editor." MUNCIE MORNING STAR,
        5 July 1944, p. 7.

        Examines Martin's article (see item 145) and
        concedes it is a fair assessment.

147.   Steele, Walter S. "Visit Middletown of the
        U.S.A." NATIONAL REPUBLIC 32 (December 1944):
        13-14, 31.

        Review of "Planning for Postwar and the Future of
        Muncie" (see item 144). Argues its usefulness as
        model for other similar-sized cities.

1946

148.   Martin, John Bartlow. "Middletown Revisited:
        Snapshots of Muncie at Peace." HARPER'S MAGAZINE
        193 (August 1946): 111-19.

        Reporter returning at end of war finds Muncie doing
        well: banks in good shape, low unemployment, greater
        social mobility. Concern expressed about postwar
        housing shortage and potential labor unrest.

1947

149.   Mayer, Frederick. "Middletown's Split Personality."
        SOCIAL STUDIES 38 (May 1947): 195-98.

        Sees Middletown as indicative of post-war America,
        with "conflict between ideal and actuality, between
        business and religion, and between the past and the
        present."

1951

150.   "Middletown's Broker." FORBES 68 (15 July 1951): 15-16.

        Interviews Muncie's only hometown broker, Kenneth J.
        Brown, while examining national trend toward small
        individual transactions in stock sales.

1952

151.   Lubell, Samuel. THE FUTURE OF AMERICAN POLITICS. New
        York: Harper, 1952.

        Describes business/labor attitudes in Muncie of
        early 1930s, and 1936 shift to Democrats, in chapter
        entitled "Revolt of the City."

1953

152.   Curti, Merle, ed. AMERICAN SCHOLARSHIP IN THE TWENTIETH
        CENTURY. 58. Cambridge: Harvard University Press,
        1953.

        Credits Lynds with furthering growth of empirical
        study of the social sciences.

1955

153.   Arensberg, Conrad M. "American Communities."
        AMERICAN ANTHROPOLOGIST 57 (December 1955): 1143-62.

        Includes discussion of Lynd and other studies of
        industrial communities, within context of historical
        overview of community patterns in United States.

1957

154.   Gillin, John. "The Application of Anthropological
        Knowledge to Modern Mass Society: An
        Anthropologist's View." HUMAN ORGANIZATION 15
        (Winter 1957): 24-29.

        Includes discussion of Lynds' Middletown
        investigations as early example of "'ethnologizing'
        of modern communities by anthropological methods,"
        later emulated in numerous other local/community
        studies, including some from Europe.

1958

155.   Gordon, Milton M. SOCIAL CLASS IN AMERICAN
        SOCIOLOGY. Durham, N.C.: Duke University Press,
        1958.

        Includes chapter "Social Class in Middletown,"
        focusing on Lynds' occupationally-based distinctions
        between working and business classes.

1959

156.   Polsby, Nelson W. "The Sociology of Community
        Power: A Reassessment." SOCIAL FORCES 37 (March
        1959): 232-36.

        Finds that "elitists" of Lynds' Middletown studies
        were not all-powerful in community decisions, citing
        example of controversial cleaning of White River
        that ended as power struggle between business and
        labor classes.

1960

157.   Stein, Maurice R. "The Lynds and Industrialization in
        Middletown." In THE ECLIPSE OF COMMUNITY: AN
        INTERPRETATION OF AMERICAN STUDIES, 47-69.
        Princeton, N.J.: Princeton University Press, 1960.

        Examines relationship of industrialization to
        urbanization, comparing Lynds studies with Robert
        Park's findings on Chicago. Other scattered
        references to Middletown throughout volume.

158.   Gordon, Whitney M. MIDDLETOWN AND IMPINGING
        FORCES (Sound Recording). Muncie, Indiana:
        Ball State University, 10 February 1960.

        Ball State sociologist discusses influence of WW II,
        the media, and politics in Muncie. Talks of
        college's impact on community and pressures within
        the college itself. Compares various responses from
        Muncie citizens regarding their feelings about Lynd
        studies.

1960

159.   Polsby, Nelson W. "Power in Middletown: Fact and Value
       in Community Research." CANADIAN JOURNAL OF
       ECONOMICS AND POLITICAL SCIENCE 4 (November 1960):
       592-603.

       Uses reissue of MIDDLETOWN as occasion to reexamine
       Lynds' treatment of community power. Suggests their
       approach may have led later studies to equate power
       elite with businessmen, ignoring influence of local
       politicians. Also finds tendency to overemphasize
       covert use of power, in effect supporting
       "conspiracy theory of elite rule."

1961

160.   Cavnes, Max Parvin. THE HOOSIER COMMUNITY AT WAR.
       Social Sciences Series, no. 20. Bloomington, Ind.:
       Indiana University Press, 1961.

       Discusses racial feelings, employment, venereal
       disease and prostitution during and after World War
       II in Arthur and Mary Lynd's [sic] "typical American
       city."

161.   Barber, Bernard. "Family Status, Local-Community
       Status, and Social Stratification: Three Types of
       Social Ranking." PACIFIC SOCIOLOGICAL REVIEW 4
       (Spring 1961): 3-10.

       Draws upon Lynds' examples of X and Y families in
       discussion of social class position, family status
       and local-community status. Suggests that conceptual
       refinement and related research is needed.

1962

162.   Gordon, Whitney H. "Stress and the Jewish Community of
        Middletown." Ph.D. diss., Purdue University, 1962.

        Describes Middletown's Jews as relatively
        prosperous, socially isolated, internally divided by
        factional disagreements, and torn between commitment
        to heritage and desire to be accepted and integrated
        into larger community. Patterns form and content of
        analysis after Lynd studies.

163.   Lipman, Eugene J., and Albert Vorspan, eds.
        A TALE OF TEN CITIES: THE TRIPLE GHETTO IN AMERICAN
        RELIGIOUS LIFE. New York: Union of American Hebrew
        Congregations, 1962.

        Chapter entitled "Muncie - Middletown in Slow
        Motion" investigates local discrimination against
        Jews, including housing restrictions, exclusion from
        clubs and organizations, and religion in schools.
        Sees some evidence of inter-religious cooperation
        but no rapid change.

164.   Madge, John. THE ORIGINS OF SCIENTIFIC SOCIOLOGY. New
        York: Free Press of Glencoe, 1962.

        Includes extended critique of Lynds' Middletown work
        in chapter entitled "Life in a Small Town." Focuses
        on methodology and mode of description.

165.   "An Oak Falls." NEWSWEEK 29 January 1962, pp. 68-70.

        Reflects upon closing of Ball glassmaking plant in
        Muncie, and describes Ball family's role as X-family
        in Lynd's Middletown studies.

166.   "Intolerance Not Respectable in Muncie, but It Is
        Present: 'Middletown in Slow Motion.'" MUNCIE
        EVENING PRESS, 11 August 1962, p. 5.

        Discusses Lipman and Vorspan findings (see item 163)
        concerning different religions and tensions among
        Catholics, Jews, and Protestants in Muncie.

1963

167.   Rossi, Peter H. "Middle-sized American City at
        Mid-Century." LIBRARY QUARTERLY 33, 1 (1963):
        3-13.

        Argues substantial change in America since Lynd
        studies and offers typology of middle-sized cities,
        with differentiation according to economic bases,
        demographic composition, and dependence on major
        metropolitan areas.

168.   Warren, Roland L. THE COMMUNITY IN AMERICA. Chicago:
        Rand McNally, 1963.

        Compares Middletown to other cities during
        Depression in a section entitled "Four American
        Communities and 'The Great Change.'"

169.   Parkinson, Leon. "Editor's Corner." MUNCIE
        EVENING PRESS, 18 July 1963, p. 4.

        Reflects upon angry Muncie reaction to MIDDLETOWN,
        but more favorable response to MIDDLETOWN IN
        TRANSITION. Notes Robert Lynd to speak at Ball
        State, probably February 1964.

170.   "Robert Lynd of 'Middletown' Fame, Nobel Winner
        Headline BSC Convos." MUNCIE STAR, 15 September
        1963, sec. D, p. 1.

        Short note on February Lynd convocation lecture.

171.   "Sociologist Sets Ball State Talk." INDIANAPOLIS STAR,
        19 September 1963, p. 44.

        Notes that Robert Lynd will present a lecture at
        Ball State Teachers College in February.

1964

172.   Gordon, Whitney M. A COMMUNITY IN STRESS. New
        York: Living Books, 1964.

        Ball State sociologist looks at small Jewish
        community in Muncie and impact of predominantly
        Protestant community upon it. Based on Ph.D.
        dissertation (see item 162).

173.   Thernstrom, Stephan. POVERTY AND PROGRESS:
        SOCIAL MOBILITY IN A NINETEENTH CENTURY CITY.
        Cambridge, Mass.: Harvard University Press, 1964.

        Chapter "Newburyport and the Larger Society"
        includes discussion of Middletown studies, arguing
        against Lynds' "blocked mobility hypothesis."

174.   "'Middletown' Author Cancels Campus Talk." MUNCIE STAR,
        17 January 1964, p. 20.

        Robert Lynd's February speech cancelled for health
        reasons. States that he would not have picked
        Muncie for study had he foreseen influence on the
        college's community.

175.   DeKadt, Emmanuel J. REVIEW OF MIDDLETOWN IN TRANSITION.
        BRITISH JOURNAL OF SOCIOLOGY 15 (December 1964):
        369-71.

        Notes reissuance of study in paperback, arguing its
        description of class articulation and local power
        structure remains forceful despite subsequent
        advances in data manipulation.

1965

176.   "'Middletown,' 'Yankee City' to be Compared." MUNCIE
        EVENING PRESS, 22 June 1965, p. 18.

        Reports that Syracuse and Harvard graduate students
        supervising Muncie survey team, results to be
        compared with similar project for Newburyport, Mass.
        H. Douglas Price, professor of political science and
        government at Syracuse and Harvard is project
        director.

177.   "Students will Conduct Survey in Muncie." MUNCIE STAR,
        23 June 1965, p. 11.

        Ball State students to assist in Syracuse/Harvard
        study. Director H. Douglas Price to include
        findings in forthcoming book.

178.   "What Do You Think of Muncie?" MUNCIE EVENING PRESS, 24
        June 1965, p. 6.

        Photo of Ball State University students assisting in
        Syracuse University study.

179.   Hiatt, Carolyn. "'Middletown' Books Resulted in
        Furor: But Few Read Them." MUNCIE STAR, 4 July
        1965, sec. A, p. 6.

        Reflects upon Lynd studies and subsequent
        investigations. Concludes that many Muncie
        residents' criticisms of Lynds' conclusions were
        based upon superficial reading or comments from
        others.

1966

180.   Barber, Bernard. "Family Status, Local-Community
        Status, and Social Stratification: Three Types of
        Social Ranking." In PERSPECTIVES ON THE AMERICAN
        COMMUNITY, edited by Roland L. Warren, 266-79.
        Chicago: Rand McNally & Company, 1966.

        Reprint of item 161.

1966

181.   Wilson, William E. INDIANA: A HISTORY. Bloomington,
        Ind.: Indiana University Press, 1966.

        Discusses Middletown in context of chapter on
        literature of Indiana. Deplores dubious reputation
        the studies brought.

182.   Gordon, Whitney H. "Jews and Gentiles in Middletown -
        1961." AMERICAN JEWISH ARCHIVES 18 (April 1966):
        41-70.

        From chapter "Middletown's Adult Jews and Non-Jews,"
        in A COMMUNITY IN STRESS (see item 162).

183.   Sinha, Surajit. "Religion in an Affluent Society."
        CURRENT ANTHROPOLOGY 7 (April 1966): 189-195.

        Report on fieldwork in American village of
        "Mapletown," located in the Midwest. Highly
        reminiscent of Lynds' work, which is cited.

1967

184.   Giel, Lawrence. "George R. Dale: Crusader for
        Free Speech and a Free Press." Ed.D. thesis, Ball
        State University, 1967.

        Notes prominence of Dale, Muncie mayor-editor, in
        both Lynd studies.

185.   Glaab, Charles N., and A. Theodore Brown. A HISTORY OF
        URBAN AMERICA. New York: Macmillan, 1967.

        Sees MIDDLETOWN as landmark study, not so much due
        to its conclusions which are seen neither as
        startling nor wide-ranging, but because it drew
        attention to "the extent and complexity of the task
        confronting social science."

1967

186.   Lingeman, Richard R.   "Middletown Now."   NEW YORK TIMES
       BOOK REVIEW, 26 February 1967, pp. 1, 22, 24, 26.

       Based upon local library circulation and bookstore
       sales statistics, native Hoosier reports
       substantial, though not surprisingly large, market
       for mass paperbacks, many of sex-adventure type, and
       general increase in interest for non-fiction, as
       compared to Lynds' 1920s findings.

187.   McFadden, Ruth M.   "McFadden Says...."   MUNCIE EVENING
       PRESS, 3 March 1967, p. 8.

       Includes excerpts from Lingeman article (see item
       186).

188.   Greene, Dick.   "New York Times Takes a Look at
       'Middletown' Reading Habits."   MUNCIE STAR, 5 March
       1967, sec. D, p. 1.

       Quotes extensively from Lingeman article (see item
       186) and notes Muncie's popularity as test market
       for everything from dog food to disposal diapers.

189.   "A Look at Us."   MUNCIE STAR, 7 March 1967, sec. 1,
       p. 4.

       Further comments on Lingeman's article (see item
       186).

1968

190.   Domer, Marilyn A.   "The Development of Federated
       Fundraising in Muncie, Indiana, 1925-57."   Ph.D.
       diss., Ball State University, 1968.

       Includes discussion of increased Ball family
       dominance in Muncie during Depression, with frequent
       reference to Lynd studies.

1968

191.   Thernstrom, Stephan. "Notes on the Historical Study of
        Social Mobility." COMPARATIVE STUDIES IN SOCIETY
        AND HISTORY, 10 (January 1968): 162-72.

        Argues that the blocked-mobility hypothesis of Lynds
        and others, seen as illustration of status
        degradation of industrialization, is oversimplified.

192.   Haines, Edmund. "Music in 'Middletown' - Not So
        Average." HIGH FIDELITY 18 (August 1968):
        MA-18, 30.

        Composer visiting Muncie to hear premiere of own
        work played by local symphony orchestra, feels that
        musically the city has outgrown its average,
        Middletown image.

193.   Hannaford, John. "Middletown, U.S.A.: Is Muncie
        Still Typical American City? Professor Looks at His
        Community." MUNCIE STAR, 10 September 1968, sec. 3,
        p. 7.

        Finds Muncie still close to national norms in many
        respects, including increased federal presence and
        corporate decision-making controlled from larger
        metropolitan centers. Muncie not so typical in its
        high unemployment, slow accumulation of social
        capital in post-WWII period, and general lack of
        planning.

1969

194.   Crowder, Daniel B. "Profile in Progress: A History of
        Local 287, UAW-CIO." Ph.D. diss., Ball State
        University, 1969.

        Relies heavily on Lynd studies and oral interviews
        dealing with history of organized labor in Muncie
        through period of Depression.

1969

195.   Yellis, Kenneth A. "Prosperity's Child: Some Thoughts
        on the Flapper." AMERICAN QUARTERLY 21 (Spring
        1969): 44-64.

        Includes discussion of 1920s dress, as described in
        MIDDLETOWN.

196.   "In 'Middletown' Money Doesn't Go Far Enough." NEW YORK
        TIMES, 24 April 1969, sec. 1, p. 49.

        Reports Muncie complaints about inflation during
        time of prosperity, especially in terms of rising
        food costs, clothing and property taxes.

197.   Gordon, Whitney H. "Middletown U.S.A. and Good
        Architecture: Fake Colonial and Ticky-tack Invade
        American Cities." TRANSACTION 6 (May 1969):
        39-42, 63.

        Compares architecture in two Indiana towns:
        Columbus and Muncie. Looks at sociological bases
        for design choices and community regard for those
        choices.

1970

198.   Downs, Robert B. BOOKS THAT CHANGED AMERICA,
        New York: Macmillan, 1970.

        Identifies MIDDLETOWN and MIDDLETOWN IN TRANSITION,
        pioneer works in social anthropology, as two of
        twenty-five titles greatly affecting American
        reading public.

199.   Lingeman, Richard R. DON'T YOU KNOW THERE'S A
        WAR ON?: THE AMERICAN HOME FRONT, 1941-1945. New
        York: G.P. Putnam's Sons, 1970.

        Includes description of Munsonians' negative
        reaction to "hillbilly" migrants and some employers'
        preference to hire blacks rather than women since
        greater percentage of latter quit jobs.

1970

200.   "TV Crew Films BSU Dissenters." MUNCIE EVENING
        PRESS, 5 February 1970, p. 5.

        Describes NBC news investigation of Middletown,
        including segment on BSU students going to
        Indianapolis anti-war rally.

201.   Creech, Floyd. "NBC to Telecast Series on Muncie."
        MUNCIE EVENING PRESS, 20 February 1970, pp. 1, 2.

        Notes choice of Muncie as typical, midwestern city
        for series on grassroots attitudes to national
        issues. Huntley-Brinkley spokesman warns that
        segments may be pre-empted and shown later if late
        breaking news intervenes.

202.   "NBC Ready With Six Segments on Muncie." MUNCIE
        STAR, 21 February 1970, p. 11.

        Huntley-Brinkley Report to include six segments, on
        generation gap, drugs, attitudes of the "silent
        majority," moratorium activities and racial
        problems.

203.   "Muncie Goes on NBC's 'Chet and Dave' Show."
        BALL STATE DAILY NEWS, 23 February 1970, p. 8.

        Discusses content of segments and lists local
        residents interviewed.

204.   Burgess, Dale. "Muncie not Middletown, USA: It
        Never Was, Even in Book." MUNCIE EVENING PRESS, 8
        April 1970, pp. 1, 5.

        Argues against Muncie's label as "typical," since
        average-sized Midwestern towns during twenties were
        products of national corporations, but Muncie was
        supported by locally-owned factories.

1970

205.   Loy, Bob. "Co-author of Famed 'Middletown' Dead:
         Made Sociological Study Here." MUNCIE EVENING
         PRESS, 3 November 1970, pp. 1, 2.

         Notes Robert Lynd's death on 1 November 1970,
         including short review of his life and work in
         Muncie.

206.   Whitman, Alden. "Robert S. Lynd, Co-author of
         'Middletown,' Dies: Sociologist's Book was 1st Major
         Profile of U. S. City." NEW YORK TIMES, 3 November
         1970, sec. 1, p. 38.

         Gives brief synopsis of Lynd's life, with discussion
         of MIDDLETOWN, hailed as first attempt to gain
         complete understanding of modern American city.

207.   "'Middletown' Sociologist Lynd Dead." MUNCIE
         STAR, 4 November 1970, p. 6.

         Discusses Lynd's Middletown fame, noting last visit
         to Muncie in 1941. Recounts that he later said he
         would not have chosen Muncie had he realized growing
         impact of Ball State on the community.

208.   Parkinson, Leon. "Editor's Corner." MUNCIE
         EVENING PRESS, 4 November 1970, p. 4.

         Eulogizes Lynd, stating initial dissatisfaction with
         MIDDLETOWN's portrayal of Muncie, but later
         realization of its accuracy. Notes that first met
         Lynd in 1924 when researchers used MUNCIE EVENING
         PRESS newsrooms as one of their headquarters.

209.   "Lynd Obituary Is Criticized." MUNCIE EVENING
         PRESS, 6 November 1970, p. 16.

         Reports that local officials and professors deny NEW
         YORK TIMES claim (see item 206) that Middletown
         books not used at Ball State University.

1970

210.   "Ball State Says 'Middletown' Is Used in Sociology
        Courses: Reply to 'Times' Obituary." MUNCIE STAR, 6
        November 1970, p. 6.

        Ball State sociology professors describe ways in
        which Lynd studies used in their courses, including
        examination of family structure and community
        decision-making processes.

211.   Greene, Dick. "Seen and Heard in Our Neighborhood."
        MUNCIE STAR, 7 November 1970, p. 4.

        Discusses unobtrusive and quiet way that Lynds lived
        while in Muncie. Includes excerpts from letters by
        Robert Lynd about Muncie.

212.   Whitman, Alden. "'Middletown' Revisited: Still
        in Transition." NEW YORK TIMES, 3 December 1970,
        sec. L, pp. 49, 95.

        Compares contemporary Muncie to community described
        in MIDDLETOWN, noting changes such as growing
        influence of Ball State and changing attitudes about
        marriage and unionization.

1971

213.   Bell, Colin, and Howard Newby. COMMUNITY STUDIES: AN
        INTRODUCTION TO THE SOCIOLOGY OF THE LOCAL
        COMMUNITY. London: George Allen and Unwin, 1971.

        Includes chapter entitled "The American Community
        Studies," with lengthy discussion of Lynds'
        methodology serving as model for later sociological
        analysis of communities.

1971

214.   Clausen, John A. Review of CLASS AND PERSONALITY
        IN SOCIETY, edited by Alan L. Grey (Atherton, 1969).
        PSYCHIATRY 34 (May 1971): 228-30.

        Includes discussion of Lynds' early influence and
        investigations of class differences upon child-
        rearing practices.

215.   "Exclusionary Zoning and Equal Protection."
        HARVARD LAW REVIEW 84 (May 1971): 1645-69.

        Includes discussion of class discrimination, citing
        Lynd findings regarding disdain of business class
        toward working class.

1972

216.   Calahan, Sean, ed.   THE PHOTOGRAPHS OF MARGARET
        BOURKE-WHITE. New York: New York Graphic Society,
        1972.

        Includes images from LIFE photo-essay on Middletown
        (see item 96). Bibliography of published
        photographs places Muncie assignment in larger
        perspective of Bourke-White's career, spanning more
        than four decades.

217.   Canty, Donald. "Reconsideration: Middletown."
        NEW REPUBLIC 166 (29 January 1972): 31-32.

        Reviews paperback editions of both Middletown
        studies. After initial reaction that they are dated
        and a product of their time, finds them still
        relevant, particularly in terms of showing continued
        need of national leadership to provide impetus for
        local, metropolitan, change.

1972

218.   Brownell, Blaine A. "A Symbol of Modernity: Attitudes
        Toward the Automobile in Southern Cities in the
        1920s." AMERICAN QUARTERLY 24 (March 1972): 20-44.

        Cites Lynd findings regarding ever-increasing
        importance of automobile, even during Depression, as
        evidence of larger national trend.

219.   Hall, Linda. "Fashion and Style in the Twenties:
        The Change." HISTORIAN 34 (May 1972): 485-97.

        Examines garment industry, including Lynds' findings
        regarding correlation between expensive stylish
        clothes and status, especially at high school level.

220.   McFadden, Ruth M. "Middletown, USA," MUNCIE EVENING
        PRESS, 29 November 1972, p. 15.

        Note on 35th anniversary of Margaret Bourke-White's
        visit to Muncie, prompted by publication of
        MIDDLETOWN IN TRANSITION.

221.   Murphy, J. Bernard. "The Faculty Intellectual in
        an Emerging University." UNIVERSITIES QUARTERLY 27
        (Winter 1972): 32-39.

        Examines pressures exerted against faculty
        intellectual at "Middlestate" University, located in
        same part of country as Middletown, in community
        with similar sub-culture, exhibiting number of anti-
        intellectual characteristics.

1973

222.   Perrigo, Lynn I. THE PROCESS OF LEARNING. Las
        Vegas: Privately printed, 1973.

        Autobiography of one-time Muncie teacher who
        provided Lynds with data on influence of Ball
        family, prior to publication of MIDDLETOWN IN
        TRANSITION.

1973

223.   Kneeland, Douglas E. "Watergate Is Remote to
        Muncie." NEW YORK TIMES, 25 April 1973, sec. 1,
        p. 24.

        Interviews cross-section of Muncie residents, seen
        as representative of "good chunk" of America,
        finding them generally tired of Watergate affair and
        more interested in jobs and prices.

224.   Passigli, Stefano. "On Power, Its Intensity and
        Distribution." EUROPEAN JOURNAL OF POLITICAL
        RESEARCH, 1 (June 1973): 163-77.

        Refers to Lynds' work as representative of the
        elitist school of community power studies, which
        assumes that unequal distribution of resources
        (wealth, education, social status) results in
        similar unequal distribution of political power.

225.   Greene, Dick. "Seen and Heard in Our
        Neighborhood." MUNCIE STAR, 6 June 1973, p. 4.

        Notes that slogan "Muncie, the Typical City" not
        used by Lynds although their study resulted in
        numerous such references to Muncie in newspapers and
        on television. Cites examples.

226.   "Study of Choice and Change in Muncie Funded."
        MUNCIE STAR, 16 December 1973, sec. A, p. 1.

        Discusses proposed 1974 study, by five Ball State
        faculty members, of public policy choices in Muncie
        and their effects.

1974

227.   Frank, Carrolyle M. "Politics in Middletown: A
        Reconsideration of Municipal Government and
        Community Power in Muncie, Indiana, 1925-1935."
        Ph.D. diss., Ball State University, 1974.

        Questions Lynds' "elitist" theory that Muncie ruled
        by oligarchy led by "X" (Ball) family. Also
        examines unusual level of corruption in Muncie
        government and career of muck-raking journalist and
        mayor, George R. Dale.

228.   Helphand, Kenneth I. "Communal Environments of Muncie."
        In MIDDLETOWN MAN, 47-56. Muncie, Ind.: Ball State
        University, 1974.

        Investigates select aspects of Muncie's environment
        - its porches, downtown, beauty parlors and bowling
        alleys.

229.   Lawbaugh, William. "Night Walk Into the 'Great
        Warm Heart': Imaginative Life in Muncie, Indiana."
        In MIDDLETOWN MAN, 31-45. Muncie, Ind.: Ball State
        University, 1974.

        Personal view of Muncie's nocturnal side - drive-
        ins, greasy spoons with linoleum counters, and
        customers perusing magazine racks of 24-hour grocery
        stores.

230.   Mammola, Joseph L. "Middletown Revisited." In
        MIDDLETOWN MAN, 3. Muncie, Ind.: Ball State
        University, 1974.

        Preface, noting that following essays "set out to
        examine the humanistic assumptions which have
        underlain the American experience as evidenced in
        the Lynds' Middletown studies."

231.   MIDDLETOWN MAN: THE HUMAN SIDE OF LIFE IN
        MUNCIE, INDIANA. Muncie, Ind.: Ball State
        University, 1974.

        Series of essays, with study questions and selected
        readings.

1974

232.   Trimmer, Joseph F. "The Quest for Community in
        America." In MIDDLETOWN MAN, 18-29. Muncie, Ind.:
        Ball State University, 1974.

        Places Lynd studies in historical context of
        American search for ideal of community.

233.   Vander Hill, C. Warren. "Middletown: Some
        Reflections on the Historical Process." In
        MIDDLETOWN MAN, 5-16. Muncie, Ind.: Ball State
        University, 1974.

        Provides overview of Muncie in late 19th century and
        during 1920s-1930s, as described by Lynds.

234.   Wilson, William H. COMING OF AGE: URBAN AMERICA,
        1915-1945. New York: John Wiley & Sons, 1974.

        Describes importance of Lynd studies, in chapter
        entitled "Cities Analyzed," but notes Middletown not
        typical of manufacturing cities or even many small
        Midwestern cities. Also suggests Lynds overstated
        case of rapid change in 1890-1924 period.

235.   Sneden, Lawrence E. "Factors Affecting the
        Mobility-orientation of the Poor." PACIFIC
        SOCIOLOGICAL REVIEW 17 (January 1974): 60-82.

        Includes reference to Lynd studies in discussion of
        lower-lower class isolation.

236.   Jones, Sally. "Muncie - A Little Something for
        Everybody." MUNCIE EVENING PRESS, 16 March 1974,
        p. 2.

        Describes, for those interested in knowing how
        Middletown residents spend their leisure time, some
        alternatives listed in local Chamber of Commerce
        brochure.

1974

237.   "'Middletown Man' Is Forum Topic at University."
       MUNCIE EVENING PRESS, 11 April 1974 p. 14.

       Four Ball State professors to lead series of public
       discussions on local reactions to Middletown studies
       and ways in which Muncie should change.

238.   Bales, Gail. "Four Humanists Turn Muncie's
       Gaze to Middletown Again: Community Invited to
       Saturday Conference." MUNCIE STAR, 14 April 1974,
       sec. C, p. 7.

       Announces Saturday conference (20 April 1974) at
       Ball State covering such topics as public policy
       choices, residents' feelings about Muncie, history
       of Ball family, and growth of Ball State University.
       Conference seen as first step in organizing for
       future Middletown III project.

239.   Walker, Brian. "What Makes Muncie Tick? Study
       Asks." MUNCIE EVENING PRESS, 20 April 1974, p. 1.

       Reports on "Middletown Man" seminar, including
       various discussion group responses. Notes, for
       example, that Archie Bunker named most often as
       television character exemplifying average Muncie
       citizen.

240.   Bell, Colin. "Replication and Reality or, The
       Future of Sociology." FUTURES 6 (June 1974): 253-60.

       Includes discussion of Lynds' functionalist approach
       in MIDDLETOWN vs influence of Marxist theory in
       MIDDLETOWN IN TRANSITION.

241.   Goheen, Peter G. "Interpreting the American
       City: Some Historical Perspectives." GEOGRAPHICAL
       REVIEW 64 (July 1974): 362-84.

       Overview of urban history approaches, with
       discussion of Lynds' work as symptomatic of the
       "local history" school which insufficiently examined
       impact of external forces upon local community
       events.

1974

242.   Freedman, Estelle B. "The New Woman: Changing
       Views of Women in the 1920s." JOURNAL OF AMERICAN
       HISTORY 61 (September 1974): 372-92.

       Notes Lynds' discussion of influence of increased
       numbers of working women during Depression upon
       traditional female roles.

243.   Yager, Florence. "Dissertation Alters Middletown
       Concept. Muncie: 1925-35." MUNCIE STAR, 3 November
       1974, sec. C, p. 8.

       Examines Frank's "Politics in Middletown...," (see
       item 227), which discusses power structure and
       corruption in Muncie. Draws comparisons with
       Watergate.

1975

244.   Smothers, David. "Muncie Still Middletown?"
       INDIANAPOLIS NEWS, 30 December 1975, sec. 1,
       pp. 1, 5.

       UPI story, investigating local developments "as a
       sort of litmus paper demonstration of Midwest
       mood...." Notes renewed hopefulness brought on by
       upturn in economy and apathy about Vietnam and
       Watergate issues.

245.   Coben, Stanley. "The Assault on Victorianism in
       the Twentieth Century." AMERICAN QUARTERLY 27
       (December 1975): 604-25.

       Notes pessimistic view of many 1920s sociological
       studies, including Lynds' Muncie, Indiana which
       "seemed like a stopping point along the way to
       Dante's Inferno."

1976

246.   Condran, John G. "Differences Between One's
        'Ideal' and One's Real Work Situation as a Measure
        of Job Satisfaction." In WORKING IN MIDDLETOWN,
        100-11. [Muncie, Ind.: Ball State University,
        1976].

        Analyzes techniques of assessing job satisfaction,
        noting that direct questioning often is inadequate
        and threatening. Suggests instead that researchers
        look at differences between respondents' actual job
        and their perception of what an ideal job might be.

247.   Condran, John G., Dwight W. Hoover, Bruce F. Meyer,
        J. Paul Mitchell, and C. Warren Vander Hill.
        WORKING IN MIDDLETOWN: GETTING A LIVING IN MUNCIE,
        INDIANA. [Muncie, Ind.: Ball State University,
        1976].

        Collection of essays and interviews from Indiana
        Committee for the Humanities project, inspired by
        Lynd studies and Studs Terkel's WORKING.

248.   "Excerpts from Interviews." In WORKING IN
        MIDDLETOWN, 6-22. [Muncie, Ind.: Ball State
        University, 1976].

        Short selections from project's transcripts.

249.   "Group Session of Five Project Humanists." In WORKING
        IN MIDDLETOWN, 23-50. [Muncie, Ind.: Ball State
        University, 1976].

        Transcripts of meeting concerned with evaluating
        project methodology and findings.

250.   Hoover, Dwight W. "An Historical Overview of
        Work in Society." In WORKING IN MIDDLETOWN, 59-88.
        [Muncie, Ind.: Ball State University, 1976].

        Includes section on "Work in Muncie," with
        discussion of development of organized labor, Ball
        family's attitudes toward workers, and Lynds'
        findings.

1976

251.   Meyer, Bruce F. "The Work Environment: An
       Editorial." In WORKING IN MIDDLETOWN, 89-99.
       [Muncie, Ind.: Ball State University, 1976].

       Examines importance of physical and psychological
       factors of work environment in determining job
       satisfaction.

252.   Mitchell, J. Paul. "Comparisons of Some Attitudes toward
       Work in Muncie, the 1930s and the 1970s." In WORKING
       IN MIDDLETOWN, 51-58. [Muncie, Ind.: Ball State
       University, 1976].

       Interviews factory workers, concluding that in 1970s
       hours generally were shorter, wages higher, working
       conditions safer and less physically demanding than
       in 1930s. By 1970s workers had higher expectations;
       fewer came from farm backgrounds.

253.   Mitchell, J. Paul. "Introduction" to WORKING IN
       MIDDLETOWN, 3-5. [Muncie, Ind.: Ball State
       University, 1976].

       Discusses impetus for study, coming from continued
       interest in issues raised earlier in MIDDLETOWN MAN
       (see item 231). Also describes interview process
       and public forums held in conjunction with project.

254.   Stoeckel, Althea L. "Laboratory Class for the
       Study of 'Middletown' and Its Environment."
       TEACHING HISTORY: A JOURNAL OF METHODS 1, 2 (1976):
       61-64.

       Ball State history professor describes course that
       examines community history through nineteenth
       century local government records.

255.   Thornburg, Thomas. SATURDAY TOWN AND OTHER POEMS.
       Georgetown, Cal.: Dragon's Teeth Press, 1976.

       Poetry by Ball State English professor and lifelong
       Middletown resident, exploring lives and feelings of
       Muncie inhabitants.

1976

256.   Colson, Elizabeth. "Culture and Progress." AMERICAN
        ANTHROPOLOGIST 78 (June 1976): 261-71.

        Sixth Distinguished Lecture, delivered before annual
        meeting of American Anthropological Association in
        1975. Discussion of history and future of the
        profession includes reference to Lynds' masking of
        Middletown's identity and ethical questions
        surrounding collection and use of data.

257.   Kohn, Melvin L. "Social Class and Parental Values:
        Another Confirmation of the Relationship." AMERICAN
        SOCIOLOGICAL REVIEW 41 (June 1976): 538-45.

        Notes that class-values relationship initially
        described by Lynds in MIDDLETOWN and since then
        reconfirmed and extended by others, including
        author.

258.   Smothers, David. "Something Happened in Muncie
        Week before Primary. Campaign '76: Report from
        Middletown, U.S.A." MUNCIE STAR, 11 July 1976,
        sec. D, p. 1.

        UPI story, focusing on surprisingly large voter
        turnout for presidential primary.

259.   Johnson, Betty. "Middletown Stars Again: This
        Time as Documentary on Finnish TV." MUNCIE EVENING
        PRESS, 21 August 1976, p. 2.

        Director of Finnish film crew "Middletown, U.S.A.,
        1976" notes interest in automotive-oriented society,
        mobile homes, recreational activities and the
        elderly.

260.   Coben, Stanley. "Foundation Officials and
        Fellowships: Innovation in the Patronage of
        Science." MINERVA 14 (Summer 1976): 225-40.

        Includes discussion of Lynd findings regarding
        importance of college education in 1920s.

1976

261.   Iliff, David. "Yes, Virginia, 'Son of Middletown' in
        Production." MUNCIE STAR, 22 September 1976, p. 1.

        Reports that four-year, National Science Foundation
        funded update of Middletown studies already has
        begun data collection phase. Discusses plans of
        project director Theodore Caplow and resident
        director Howard Bahr.

262.   "Virginia School to Do Lynd-type Study of Muncie."
        MUNCIE EVENING PRESS, 22 September 1976, p. 28.

        Gives brief background on Middletown III study,
        including source of funding and researchers.

263.   "Book Tells of Work in Middletown USA." MUNCIE
        WEEKLY NEWS, 25 November 1976, p. 3.

        Discusses WORKING IN MIDDLETOWN (item 247), by five
        Ball State professors, and their findings regarding
        job satisfaction.

1977

264.   Frank, Carrolyle M. "Muncie Politics: George R.
        Dale, Municipal Reformer, 1921-1936." In CITIES IN
        HISTORY. Vol. 1, no. 4 of CONSPECTUS OF HISTORY,
        edited by Dwight W. Hoover and John T. Koumoulides,
        34-47. Muncie, Ind.: Department of History, Ball
        State University, 1977.

        Traces career of George Dale (only person mentioned
        by name in both Middletown studies) as anti-Klan
        editor of MUNCIE POST-DEMOCRAT and mayor of Muncie.

1977

265.   Goist, Park Dixon. FROM MAIN STREET TO STATE
        STREET: TOWN, CITY AND COMMUNITY IN AMERICA. Port
        Washington, N.Y.: Kennikat Press, 1977.

        Includes chapter entitled "Middletown and the
        'Eclipse of Community': Robert and Helen Lynd,"
        which emphasizes Lynds' social anthropological
        approach to investigation of impact of urbanization
        and industrialization.

266.   Mandel, Leon. DRIVEN: THE AMERICAN FOUR-WHEELED
        LOVE AFFAIR. New York: Stein and Day, 1977.

        Notes that Lynds' discussion of the automobile
        curiously was included in leisure section although
        impact of automobile on Muncie's economy even then
        was significant. Investigates current trends such as
        unemployment in auto industry, deteriorating city
        center, endless used-car dealerships, go-kart/dirt
        bike/motor-home enthusiasts, public transportation,
        and move to suburbs.

267.   Matthews, Glenna Christine. "A California Middletown:
        The Social History of San Jose in the Depression."
        Ph.D. diss., Stanford University, 1977.

        Compares working class of San Jose and Muncie,
        arguing greater militancy in San Jose due to ethnic
        institutions of Italian cannery workers, which
        strengthened class solidarity.

268.   Frank, Carrolyle Marlin. "Middletown Revisited:
        Reappraising the Lynds' Classic Studies of Muncie,
        Indiana." INDIANA SOCIAL STUDIES QUARTERLY 30
        (Spring 1977): 94-100.

        Questions Lynds' "elitist" theory of Muncie power
        structure (controlled behind the scenes by the X-
        family), but supports their findings on municipal
        corruption Argues that Lynds oversimplified the
        political make-up of Muncie.

1977

269.   Spurgeon, Wiley. "New Research Suggests 'Middletown'
       Wasn't as Typical as Lynd Thought." MUNCIE STAR,
       30 March 1977, p. 22.

       Summarizes Rotary Club talk by Howard Bahr about
       differences in research techniques used in
       Middletown and Middletown III studies. Reflects
       upon charges that Lynds held an anti-business bias
       and romanticized pre-industrial American society.

270.   Friedman, Saul. "'Middletown U.S.A.' Withholds
       Judgement on Carter." PHILADELPHIA INQUIRER, 1 May
       1977, sec. A, pp. 1, 16.

       Finds that Muncie residents like President's style,
       lack of pretense, and criticism of Washington
       politics, but conservative Republicans and Democrats
       alike still waiting to see what actions he will
       take. Notes reason for studying local opinion is
       Middletown label and subsequent reputation as
       popular national test market.

271.   Iliff, David. "Middletown III Researchers Begin
       Study of Work Force in Muncie." MUNCIE STAR, 7
       September 1977, pp. 1, 2.

       Discusses Middletown III questionnaires and
       publication plans. Notes initial low profile due to
       researchers' uncertainty about reaction of Muncie
       residents to yet another study of their community.

272.   "'Middletown' Study Eyes City's Workers." MUNCIE
       EVENING PRESS, 7 September 1977, p. 10.

       Summarizes upcoming Middletown III research which
       will focus on work, religion and politics.

1978

273.   Bracken, Alexander E., Jr. "Middletown as a
        Pioneer Community." Ph.D. Diss., Ball State
        University, 1978.

        Examines social mobility patterns in Muncie during
        1850-1880 period, which was characterized by great
        geographic mobility. Concludes that those who
        stayed, regardless of place of birth, generally
        improved both their occupational and economic
        status.

274.   Coldwater, Charles F., M.D. COLDWATER RUNS DEEP.
        Muncie, Ind.: Privately printed, 1978.

        Chronologically organized poems, dealing with major
        events in the life of Coldwater (pseud. Philip
        Ball), Middletown's development, its residents, and
        Midwestern pride. Includes poem "Middletown,
        U.S.A."

275.   Jones, Carmel L. "Migration, Religion, and
        Occupational Mobility of Southern Appalachians in
        Muncie, Indiana." Ed.D. thesis, Ball State
        University, 1978.

        Includes analysis of negative stereotypes about
        migrants reported and accepted by Lynds, who
        apparently relied solely on second-hand information.

276.   Lynd, Helen Merrell, with the collaboration of
        Staughton Lynd. POSSIBILITIES. Youngstown, Ohio:
        Ink Well Press, c.1978; distributed by Sarah
        Lawrence College.

        Includes reminiscences on Middletown research, drawn
        from interviews conducted under auspices of Oral
        History Research Office of Columbia University.

1978

277.   "'Middletown III': Conductor of Study Hopes It Helps
        City." MUNCIE EVENING PRESS, 12 January 1978,
        p. 32.

        Bruce Chadwick comments on four-year research
        project on family, education, government, and role
        of women in labor force.

278.   Printz, John Robert. "Through a Glass Darkly:
        Value Presuppositions in the Work of Robert S.
        Lynd." Ph.D. diss., University of Minnesota, 1978.

        Includes discussion of tension in Middletown
        studies, between Lynd's desire to maintain
        objectivity and crusading spirit seeking to bring
        about social change.

279.   "Sociologist Explains Aims of 'Middletown III'
        Project." MUNCIE STAR, 12 January 1978, p. 14.

        Remarks by Chadwick, before Muncie Kiwanis Club,
        including overview of Middletown III research topics
        and survey techniques.

280.   "'Middletown' Study Forms Sent to 1,000 Muncie
        Women." MUNCIE STAR, 21 March 1978, p. 3.

        Announces that Middletown III questionnaires sent
        out regarding changing roles of women in society.

281.   "Women's Attitudes Sought in Latest 'Middletown'
        Study." MUNCIE EVENING PRESS, 21 March 1978, p. 12.

        Reports mailing of Middletown III questionnaires to
        over 1000 married and single women in Muncie,
        randomly chosen from city directory. Chadwick,
        director of study, plans to compare current results
        with those obtained by Lynds, and expects
        significant change.

1978

282.   Johnson, Steven [sic] D. "Judgments of Equity and Vote
        in a Presidential Election." SOCIOLOGICAL FOCUS 11
        (April 1978): 161-72.

        Results from stratified sample of 213 Middletown
        residents indicate tendency to vote for the 1976
        candidate "willing and capable of eliminating a
        perceived unfair advantage of an undeserving segment
        of American society."

283.   "Federal Impact Answers Sought." MUNCIE STAR,
        15 April 1978, sec. A, p. 6.

        Notes Middletown III questionnaires about federal
        spending in Muncie mailed to 500 households.

284.   "Study Questionnaires Mailed to 500 Here." MUNCIE
        EVENING PRESS, 15 April 1978, p. 7.

        Middletown III federal presence questionnaires sent
        out. Research director Chadwick seeking data on
        number of Middletown participants in federal
        programs, dollars spent, and public response.

285.   "Teen-Ager Beliefs Here Show Little Change in 50
        Years." MUNCIE EVENING PRESS, 12 June 1978, p. 1.

        Middletown III survey of teenager's attitudes and
        values, elicits near-same results as Lynds studies.
        Middletown youth still deeply Christian, pro-
        American and stronger in belief than grandparents
        concerning capitalism.

286.   Powell, Jan. "'Today' Wants to Know Why We're
        So Contented." MUNCIE STAR, 23 June 1978, p. 1.

        Reports that NBC to film segment on Muncie, in
        conjunction with examination of Middletown III
        findings that most local residents happy with their
        lifestyles.

1978

287.   Wilcox, Sue Ellen. "NBC's 'Today' to Turn Its
         Cameras on Muncie: 'The Happy People.'" MUNCIE
         EVENING PRESS, 23 June 1978, p. 2.

         Announces that NBC film crew will be in Muncie to
         seek opinions from residents about their community.

288.   Canan, Joe. "'Today' Cameras Zoom in on Muncie."
         MUNCIE EVENING PRESS, 26 June 1978, p. 1.

         Discusses interviews conducted by Eric Burns and NBC
         film crew, and expresses concern of Muncie residents
         that show may adopt condescending attitude.

289.   Canan, Joe. "Muncie's on Tomorrow's 'Today' Show."
         MUNCIE EVENING PRESS, 28 June 1978, p. 5.

         Notes departure of NBC film crew, after interviews
         with participants in original Lynd study,
         descendants of conservation club members. Shown in
         Bourke-White article, and others.

290.   Parkinson, Leon. "Our Town." MUNCIE EVENING PRESS, 28
         June 1978, p. 4.

         Reports arrival of "Today" crew and gives personal
         insights about earlier visits of Lynds and Bourke-
         White.

291.   Canon, Joe. "Most Here Like Muncie Image Presented on
         'Today' Show." MUNCIE EVENING PRESS, 29 June 1978,
         pp. 1, 2.

         Cites reactions of Muncie residents, many of whom
         expressed relief that community was not portrayed
         in negative light.

1978

292.   Spurgeon, Bill. "'Middletown' Goes Under the
        Microscope - for Happiness." MUNCIE STAR, 1 July
        1978, sec. B, p. 8.

        Reflects upon worldwide interest, most recently
        "Today" show, of those "who want to get a quick
        handle on some problem or another by seeing what the
        folks 'out there in Middletown' think about it."
        Finds many of the stories rather superficial.

293.   "BSU Research Grant Topics Announced." MUNCIE
        STAR, 6 July 1978, p. 36.

        Includes reference to grant awarded to John Hewitt
        on topic entitled "Doing Justice in Middletown," a
        study of felony sentencing patterns in Muncie.

294.   Magnusson, Paul. "Smalltown America, One More Time."
        DETROIT FREE PRESS, 9 July 1978, sec. C, pp. 1, 4.

        Describes Middletown III preliminary findings,
        supplemented by interviews with local residents.
        Suggests that slower-paced life and relative lack of
        change give illusion that community slept through
        the sixties. Knight-Ridder story, picked up by
        other papers around the country, including ANAHEIM
        REGISTER, CHICAGO TRIBUNE, and Lexington, Kentucky
        HERALD-LEADER.

295.   Spurgeon, Bill. "Seen and Heard in Our Neighborhood."
        MUNCIE STAR, 22 August 1978, p. 4.

        Notes receipt of letter from Ball State
        anthropologist, B.K. Swartz, who argues that Robert
        Lynd's application of ethnographic techniques to an
        American community distinguish him as an
        anthropologist rather than a sociologist.

1978

296.   Magnusson, Paul. "Almost Like Muncie Slept Through
        '60's." ANAHEIM (Calif.) REGISTER, 1 September
        1978, sec. C, p. 6.

        Knight-Ridder News Wire story, describes findings
        from Middletown III researchers and interviews with
        local residents, noting general satisfaction with
        slower pace of life and conservative approach to
        religion and politics.

297.   Magnusson, Paul. "Munsonians - Just Average Citizens
        Loving God, Country." CHICAGO TRIBUNE, 4 September
        1978, sec. 3, pp. 1, 4.

        Reprint of item 296.

298.   Munson, Anita. "City Goes Under TIME'S Scrutiny
        Now." MUNCIE EVENING PRESS, 29 September 1978,
        p. 1.

        Discusses visit of TIME magazine reporter Robert
        Suro and several topics of investigation including
        racial strife in the '60's and local "big news"
        stories.

299.   Melina, Lois, and Bill Spurgeon. "Hold on to Your
        Seats: 'Time' Visits Middletown." MUNCIE STAR, 11
        October 1978, pp. 1, 9.

        Criticizes article's choice of photographs, such as
        woman in pioneer dress eating corn on the cob, which
        overstates "down home" portrayal. Also points out
        that TIME only one of several recent examples of
        ongoing national media interest in Middletown.

300.   "'Middletown' Revisited." TIME, 16 October 1978, 106-8.

        Reports findings from Middletown III replication of
        Lynds' high school survey, noting persistence of
        social values, but other changes such as increased
        participation of women in labor force.

1978

301.   "Muncie's Two-income Families Scrutinized." MUNCIE
        STAR, 23 October 1978, p. 1.

        Announces MONEY magazine research team coming to
        investigate two-income families and their attitudes.
        Resulting article to be published January 1979 (see
        item 309).

302.   "Album of Yesteryear: Robert Lynd Visiting Muncie."
        MUNCIE STAR, 26 November 1978, sec. C, p. 7.

        Includes photograph of Lynd, taken in September
        1941, along with brief description of his work in
        Muncie.

303.   Baer, Diane. "Editor Finds Munsonians Have a
        Pretty Good Thing: Another Look at Our Town."
        MUNCIE EVENING PRESS, 23 December 1978, p. 2.

        Notes visit from Errol Uys, Senior Editor of
        READER'S DIGEST. Uys found Muncie in good condition
        with one problem: restless youth.

304.   Bracken, Alexander E. "Middletown before the
        Lynds: Geographical and Social Mobility in Muncie,
        1850-1880." INDIANA SOCIAL STUDIES QUARTERLY 31
        (Winter 1978-1979): 38-45.

        Argues that Muncie, like other urban communities of
        that era, experienced high degree of geographic
        mobility. Social mobility, based upon occupational
        change and property ownership, also was relatively
        open, especially in skilled and nonmanual
        categories.

1979

305.   Chappell, Craig Bradford. "The Status Attainment
        Process: Women in the Labor Force of Middletown."
        Ph.D. diss., Brigham Young University, 1979.

        Examines data from 1978 Middletown III mail
        questionnaire to 1006 women, concluding that two
        most important factors affecting status attainment
        were education and first job.

306.   Coldwater, Charles F., M.D. Report from MIDDLETOWN AND
        NORMAL CITY. Muncie, Ind.: Privately published,
        1979.

        Collection of Dr. Coldwater's (pseud. Philip Ball)
        letters to MUNCIE STAR columnist Bob Barnet and to
        MUNCIE EVENING PRESS editor Harold Trulock, A
        humorous, homespun, philosophical approach to life
        in Middletown.

307.   Leigh, Geoffrey K. "Kinship Interaction Over the
        Family Life Span." Ph.D. diss., Brigham Young
        University, 1979.

        Examines data sets from North Carolina interviews
        and Middletown III survey, concluding that
        interaction of close relatives substantially greater
        than more distant relatives, geographic distance has
        mild negative effect on interaction, and affectional
        closeness and enjoyment also influence degree of
        interaction.

308.   Szacki, Jerzy. HISTORY OF SOCIOLOGICAL THOUGHT.
        Contributions in Sociology, no. 35. Westport, Conn.:
        Greenwood Press, 1979

        Discusses ethnographic perspective of the Lynds, as
        compared to empirical research of Chicago school, in
        chapter on American descriptive sociology.

1979

309.   Scharff, Edward E. "The Two-paycheck Life: A Subtle
       Revolution." MONEY 8 (January 1979): 34, 36-39.

       Notes major change in Muncie since Lynds' studies:
       women want to work outside home. Interviews number
       of two-income families about necessity, spending
       habits and savings. Includes results of various
       Middletown III surveys.

310.   Wilcox, Sue Ellen. "'Money' Talks - About Muncie:
       Magazine Looks at Two-income Families." MUNCIE
       EVENING PRESS, 5 January 1979, pp. 1, 2.

       Discusses MONEY article (see item 309) and quotes
       Middletown III reports that women work for enjoyment
       more than for financial gain.

311.   "City to Go Under Film Scrutiny Next." MUNCIE
       EVENING PRESS, 19 January 1979, p. 1.

       Reports that three Ball State University professors
       and filmmaker Peter Davis (Producer-"Selling of the
       Pentagon") awarded grant to develop script for
       documentary about Muncie. Some details on scope of
       project given.

312.   "They'll Put 'Middletown' on Film Next." MUNCIE
       STAR, 20 January 1979, sec. B, p. 6.

       Announcement similar to item 311.

313.   Jones, Sally. "They're Checking City's Pulse
       Again." MUNCIE EVENING PRESS, 23 February 1979,
       pp. 1, 2.

       Announces that Knight-Ridder newspaper chain is
       sending reporters to Muncie to interview people on
       attitudes about federal government and Carter
       administration.

1979

314.   Caplow, Theodore, and Howard M. Bahr. "Half a
        Century of Change in Adolescent Attitudes:
        Replication of a Middletown Survey by the Lynds."
        PUBLIC OPINION QUARTERLY 43 (Spring 1979): 1-17.

        Reports results of 1977 high school survey which
        included 20 attitude items administered by Lynds in
        1924. Finds remarkable tenacity of values regarding
        religion, patriotism and Protestant ethic.

315.   Hewitt, John D., and William S. Johnson. "Dropping Out
        in 'Middletown.'" HIGH SCHOOL JOURNAL 62 (March
        1979): 252-256.

        Examines data from 1924, 1937, 1952 and 1977
        studies, concluding that "poor grades, low
        involvement in social activities and a personal
        dissatisfaction with school in general" are
        significant factors influencing dropout rate, and
        have not changed much in past 50 years.

316.   Friedman, Saul, and Frank Greve. "Another Survey: This
        One Finds Muncie 'Ungrateful.'" MUNCIE EVENING
        PRESS, 7 March 1979, pp. 1, 7, 8.

        Knight-Ridder report noting that most Munsonians
        benefit from federal funds, but think government
        spending should be cut.

317.   Friedman, Saul, and Frank Greve. "Carter in Vote
        Trouble Here in 'Middletown'?" MUNCIE EVENING
        PRESS, 8 March 1979, pp. 6, 7.

        Knight-Ridder story, comparing Muncie mayor, Robert
        Cunningham, to President Carter. Both perceived as
        honest but ineffectual political outsiders. Story
        carried by other newspapers, including HOUSTON POST.

1979

318.   Friedman, Saul, and Frank Greve. "Throw the Feds Out:
        Muncie Typical of Cities Calling for Spending
        Cutbacks." HOUSTON POST, 11 March 1979, sec. A,
        p. 3.

        Knight-Ridder story, drawing on data from own survey
        and research of Middletown III associate, Penelope
        Austin. Finds that community, despite nearly $700
        million in federal aid over last decade, favors
        spending cuts and balanced budget.

319.   White, Jane See. "Despite 50 years, Physical
        Changes, Muncie Is 'Middletown' and Glad of It."
        INDIANAPOLIS STAR, 25 March 1979, sec. 5, pp. 1, 4.

        Discusses findings of Middletown III study,
        including lack of change and apparent endurance of
        certain fundamental values and ideas. Major
        difference noted is increase in number of working
        women.

320.   White, Jane See. "'Middletown' More Cosmopolitan - But
        Parallels to '20's Study 'Spooky.'" MUNCIE STAR, 25
        March 1979, sec. D, p. 2.

        Reports Middletown III findings by Caplow, who
        argues pace of change has slowed and institutional
        patterns described by Lynds still in place.

321.   "Typical U.S. Town Keeps 1920's Values: A New Look at
        Muncie, 50 Years After Famous Study, Finds
        'Surprising' Similarities." NEW YORK TIMES, 26
        March 1979, sec. B, p. 12.

        Reports Caplow's recent findings from Middletown III
        studies, stressing lack of change from Lynds' 1920s
        studies.

1979

322.   "'Middletown' Lures Aussie Prof to BSU: Typical
        American University?" MUNCIE EVENING PRESS, 4 April
        1979, sec. 1, p. 6.

        Notes visit of Dr. William Coppell of Maquari
        University, Sydney, Australia, as part of a study of
        comparative education. Believes Ball State to be
        "representative of American universities."

323.   "'Middletown' Revisited." MUNCIE STAR, 13 April 1979,
        p. 4.

        Guest editorial, from FORT WAYNE JOURNAL GAZETTE,
        reporting that Middletown III investigation almost
        complete. Notes persistence of religious and
        patriotic beliefs, but also increased tolerance.

324.   Winters, Rita. "'Middletown' Talk Set for Historical
        Society." MUNCIE STAR, 8 May 1979, p. 7.

        Announces lecture by Ball State professor Warren
        Vander Hill on Lynd studies and Middletown III
        preliminary findings.

325.   "'Middletown' Books Topic at Historical Society
        Meeting." MUNCIE STAR, 19 May 1979, sec. A, p. 4.

        Summary of Vander Hill lecture, emphasizing
        participant-observer approach adopted by Lynds.

326.   "Side Remarks." MUNCIE STAR, 27 May 1979, sec. A,
        p. 14.

        Notes appearance of Jane See White article (see item
        320) in CLEARWATER (Fla.) SUN, but accompanied by
        sketches of businesses not existing in Muncie, such
        as A & P supermarket and topless bar.

1979

327.   Ruddick, Jeanie. "1937's Typical American Family Not So
        Typical 42 Years Later." MUNCIE STAR, 18 June 1979,
        p. 5.

        Update on Glen and Nellie Craig family, winners of
        1937 local newspaper contest, searching for "typical
        American family." Contest was response to Bourke-
        White's photo-essay in LIFE (see items 96) and
        brought Craigs national fame.

328.   "At Ball State: Movie on Muncie Set." MUNCIE STAR,
        20 June 1979, p. 15.

        Announces that Ball State professors Dwight Hoover,
        Joseph Trimmer and C. Warren Vander Hill, along with
        producer Peter Davis awarded PBS grant for
        production of documentary film about elections and
        other political processes in Muncie.

329.   "The Changing Times." FAMILY WEEKLY, 29 July 1979,
        p. 22.

        Note on Middletown III findings about working women.

330.   Munson, Anita. "'Middletown' Fame to Reach Across
        Ocean: British Mag Plans Article." MUNCIE EVENING
        PRESS, 7 August 1979, p. 1.

        Reports intentions of British magazine, NOW, to do
        piece on November presidential election, Chrysler's
        financial trouble and general state of American
        economy according to Middletowners.

331.   "Now Comes to Muncie." MUNCIE STAR, 8 August 1979,
        p. 11.

        Short notice that British reporters from NOW
        magazine in Muncie interviewing residents about
        politics and change in the community.

1979

332. Margolick, David M. "Law in 'Middletown.'" NATIONAL
LAW JOURNAL 49 (20 August 1979): 1, 14-16.

Draws portrait of lawyers in Middletown, from sons
of working-class families to sons of local elite.
Describes relaxed style of legal practices and
protocol.

333. Caplow, Theodore. "The Gradual Progress of Equality in
Middletown: A Tocquevillean Theme Re-examined." THE
TOCQUEVILLE REVIEW 1 (Fall 1979): 114-126.

Measures inequality in Middletown through use of
"Gini" ratios, as applied to shifts in family
income, educational achievement and occupational
prestige during 1920-1970 period.

334. Bohlke, Robert H. "Bibliography of Robert S. Lynd."
JOURNAL OF THE HISTORY OF SOCIOLOGY 2 (Fall-Winter
1979-1980): 128-131.

Provides chronological list of monographs and
articles, but omits MIDDLETOWN IN TRANSITION.

335. Caplow, Theodore. "The Changing Middletown
Family." JOURNAL OF THE HISTORY OF SOCIOLOGY 2
(Fall-Winter 1979-80): 66-98.

Examines aspects of Middletown social and family
life by comparing Lynds' results with Middletown III
Project survey results.

336. Engler, Robert. "Knowledge for What? Indeed."
JOURNAL OF THE HISTORY OF SOCIOLOGY 2 (Fall-Winter
1979-80): 121-26.

Pictures Lynd as outspoken man, scolding colleagues
for quietism during the 1930s.

1979

337.   Etzkowitz, Henry. "Americanization of Marx:
        MIDDLETOWN and MIDDLETOWN IN TRANSITION." JOURNAL
        OF THE HISTORY OF SOCIOLOGY 2 (Fall-Winter 1979-
        1980): 41-57.

        Argues that Lynds may not have explicitly espoused
        Marxist theory in Middletown studies but they shared
        ideals of developed class consciousness and
        organized working class, and "used Marx's method of
        analyzing the relationship between changes in the
        forces and relationships of production." Concludes
        that Middletown work "provides a groundwork for a
        reinterpretation of Marxian theory that is
        applicable to contemporary society."

338.   Lindt, Gillian. "Introduction: Robert S. Lynd:
        American Scholar-Activist." JOURNAL OF THE HISTORY
        OF SOCIOLOGY 2 (Fall-Winter 1979-80): 1-12.

        Prefatory article examining Lynd's education,
        writings and contributions to sociology.

339.   Lynd, Robert S. "Done in Oil." JOURNAL OF THE
        HISTORY OF SOCIOLOGY 2 (Fall-Winter 1979-80): 23-40.

        Describes unsatisfactory labor and living conditions
        at Elk Basin, Wyoming oil field, owned by Standard
        Oil. First published in SURVEY GRAPHIC 49, 3
        (1 November 1922).

340.   Lynd, Staughton. "Robert S. Lynd: The Elk
        Basin Experience." JOURNAL OF THE HISTORY OF
        SOCIOLOGY 2 (Fall-Winter 1979-80): 14-22.

        Discusses father's work during summer of 1921, as a
        visiting preacher in Rockefeller oil camp in Elk
        Basin, noting that two resultant articles, "Crude-
        Oil Religion" and "Done in Oil," led to invitation
        to do Middletown study.

1979

341. Miller, S. M. "Struggles for Relevance: The Lynd
      Legacy." JOURNAL OF THE HISTORY OF SOCIOLOGY, 2
      (Fall-Winter 1979-80): 58-64.

      Disagrees with Etzkowitz' contention (see item 337)
      that Middletown books represent "the Americanization
      of Marx," arguing instead that Lynd views came from
      muckraking and populist tradition.

342. Smith, Mark C. "Robert Lynd and Consumerism in
      the 1930's." JOURNAL OF THE HISTORY OF SOCIOLOGY, 2
      (Fall-Winter 1979-80): 99-120.

      Traces Lynd's increasing involvement in consumer
      issues, particularly from viewpoint of examining
      ways in which modern American capitalism has
      influenced people's needs and values. Article
      adapted from dissertation chapter entitled "Robert
      Lynd and Knowledge for What?" (See item 359).

343. Margolick, Dave. "Muncie Attorneys Are Caught in
      Middletown's 'Typical' Time Warp." MUNCIE EVENING
      PRESS, 1 September 1979, pp. 8, 9.

      Reprint of item 332.

344. Hayes, Tom. "'Middletown' Label Looked at in
      Third Study." BALL STATE DAILY NEWS (Weekend
      Supplement), 28 September 1979, pp. 9-12.

      Photo-essay describing work of Middletown III
      researchers and noting some present-day Muncie
      features, such as substantial university population,
      making it less than "typical."

1979

345.   Hoover, Dwight W. "Toward a Social History of
        Muncie." INDIANA ACADEMY OF SOCIAL SCIENCES
        PROCEEDINGS 14 (5 October 1979): 124-28.

        Examines usefulness of urban history approaches
        based on social mobility/physical mobility and
        modernization, finding neither explain adequately
        the persistence of traditional values in Muncie,
        most recently described by Middletown III
        researchers.

346.   Ball, Ellen, and Diane Baer. "Middletown Film
        Project Needs Photos, Home Movies." MUNCIE EVENING
        PRESS, 3 October 1979, p. 10.

        Announces that Ball State professor, Joe Trimmer,
        requesting loan of materials from 1920s-1940s
        period, for use in film series to be televised
        nationwide in 1981.

347.   Toolan, Sean. "Muncie - It's No Ordinary Midwest City."
        CHICAGO TRIBUNE, 30 November 1979, pp. 1, 4.

        Describes features, most notably a sizable state
        university, which cause Muncie to deviate from norm
        and consequently which would preclude its selection
        as Middletown if Lynds currently were to look for a
        research site.

348.   Caplow, Theodore. "The Measurement of Social Change in
        Middletown." INDIANA MAGAZINE OF HISTORY 75
        (December 1979): 344-57.

        Finds quantitative changes but no fundamental
        transformations of Middletown social values during
        five decades since first Lynd study. Discusses
        methods for measuring rate of modernization, noting
        deceleration from 1920s to 1970s.

1979

349.   Caplow, Theodore, and Bruce A. Chadwick. "Inequality
        and Life-Styles in Middletown, 1920-1978." SOCIAL
        SCIENCE QUARTERLY 60 (December 1979): 367-86.

        Finds that average Middletown family occupational
        levels have risen over past two generations and that
        difference in business and working class lifestyles
        generally have diminished from 1924 to 1978.

350.   Frank, Carrolyle M. "Who Governed Middletown?:
        Community Power in Muncie, Indiana, in the 1930s."
        INDIANA MAGAZINE OF HISTORY 75 (December 1979):
        321-43.

        Examines Muncie decision making-processes, finding
        Lynds' elitist approach overstated and arguing
        instead for a combination of federalist and
        pluralist models.

351.   "Introduction: 'Middletown' and Muncie." INDIANA
        MAGAZINE OF HISTORY 75 (December 1979): 301-2.

        Notes enduring impact of Lynd studies, seen as "the
        fullest and most thought provoking...of an Indiana
        community in the twentieth century."

352.   Jensen, Richard. "The Lynds Revisited." INDIANA
        MAGAZINE OF HISTORY 75 (December 1979): 303-19.

        Finds MIDDLETOWN's description of everyday life
        in small-town America of enduring value, but
        criticizes its view of a "mythic pre-industrial
        past" and its condemnation of evils of
        modernization. Argues that its conclusions regarding
        impact of industrialization upon workers compromised
        by lack of detailed analysis.

1980

353.   Bahr, Howard M., Theodore Caplow, and Geoffrey K. Leigh.
        "The Slowing of Modernization in Middletown." In
        RESEARCH IN SOCIAL MOVEMENTS, CONFLICTS AND CHANGE,
        Vol. 3, edited by L Kriesberg, 219-32. Greenwich,
        Conn.: JAI Press, 1980.

        Finds that present-day adolescents in Middletown,
        with a more stabilized population, experiencing less
        social change than 1924 counterparts.

354.   Chadwick, Bruce A., and C. Bradford Chappell. "The Two-
        Income Family in Middletown, 1924-1978." In
        ECONOMICS AND THE FAMILY, edited by Stephen J. Bahr,
        27-42. Lexington, Mass.: Lexington Books, 1980.

        Argues that main shift toward women entering labor
        force occurred between 1890 and 1920, prior to Lynd
        studies, but major change from 1920s to 1970s has
        been increase of two-income families among business
        class.

355.   Coldwater, Charles F., M.D. THE GHOST OF GAS BOOM PAST.
        Muncie, Ind.: Privately published, 1980.

        Collected poems of Dr. Coldwater (pseud. Philip
        Ball), illustrating Middletown values, attitudes and
        personal histories in a humorous vein. Title refers
        to 1890s gas boom period in Muncie's history.
        Includes "The Blues in Middletown," "The View from
        Middletown, Looking Out," and "Middletown
        Revisited."

356.   Lingeman, Richard R. SMALL TOWN AMERICA: A NARRATIVE
        HISTORY 1620 - PRESENT. New York: G.P. Putnam's
        Sons, 1980.

        Scattered references to Muncie/Middletown in work by
        native Hoosier. Examines structure and function of
        smaller communities throughout America's history.

1980

357.   Hewitt, John D. AN ENUMERATION OF CRIMINAL CHARGES
        FILED IN DELAWARE COUNTY COURTS: 1829-1900. Muncie,
        Ind.: Center for Middletown Studies, Ball State
        University, 1980.

        Lists raw data, noting that material collected as
        part of larger research project examining history of
        crime and criminal justice institutions in
        Middletown.

358.   Reed, James S. "Clark Wissler: A Forgotten Influence in
        American Anthropology." Ph.D. diss., Ball State
        University, 1980.

        Includes discussion of Wissler's foreword to
        MIDDLETOWN, noting relevant correspondence in
        Wissler Papers (held in Department of Anthropology,
        Ball State University).

359.   Smith, Mark Calvin. "Knowledge for What: Social
        Science and the Debate Over Its Role in 1930's
        America." Ph.D. diss., University of Texas at
        Austin, 1980.

        Argues emergence of two approaches to social
        science: the objectivist school, concentrating on
        sophisticated methodological techniques; and the
        purposive school, with Robert Lynd as a
        representative, arguing need to suggest desirable
        societal goals rather than merely analyzing status
        quo.

360.   Vanek, Joann. "Household Work, Wage Work, and
        Sexual Equality." In WOMEN AND HOUSEHOLD LABOR,
        275-91, edited by Sarah Fenstermaker Berk, Sage
        Yearbooks in Women's Policy Studies, Vol. 5.
        Beverly Hills: Sage, 1980.

        In section entitled "Attitudes and Work Roles,"
        finds Lynds' examination of changing family roles
        still relevant.

1980

361.   Caplow, Theodore. "Middletown Fifty Years After."
        CONTEMPORARY SOCIOLOGY 9 (January 1980): 46-50.

        Review essay, contending Middletown books still
        fresh, largely because they address vital questions
        of continuity and change in American society.
        Argues, however, that MIDDLETOWN IN TRANSITION is a
        flimsier and gloomier work. Examines Lynds'
        methodology and historical place in community
        studies, and concludes with summary of own
        Middletown III fieldwork.

362.   Hallawell, Jo Ann. "Faculty Visitors Will Exchange
        Ideas." BALL STATE DAILY NEWS, 2 February 1980,
        p. 7.

        Discusses Ball State University visit planned for
        faculty members from Western Illinois and Western
        Kentucky Universities. "Middletown" tour planned to
        highlight Muncie's unusual historical background.

363.   "'Today' Interviews City Residents." BALL STATE
        DAILY NEWS, 5 February 1980, p. 2.

        Reports arrival of Fred Briggs, "Today" show
        travelling reporter, to interview residents about
        life in "Middletown." Notes that Caplow already
        interviewed.

364.   "They Care About Us." MUNCIE STAR, 19 February
        1980, p. 8.

        Describes Canadian newspaper request for phone
        number of local bars, to interview Muncie residents
        on their opinions of the two candidates for Canadian
        prime minister in upcoming election.

365.   "Grant for Middletown Film Okayed." MUNCIE EVENING
        PRESS, 21 February 1980, p. 22.

        Announces awarding of Indiana Committee for the
        Humanities $50,000 challenge grant to Middletown
        Film Project.

1980

366. "Grant Approved." MUNCIE STAR, 22 February 1980,
          p. 19.

          Statement of Indiana Committee for the Humanities
          approval of funds to Middletown Film Project for
          six-part documentary.

367. "City's Black Population Study Topic." MUNCIE
          STAR, 28 February 1980, pp. 1, 3.

          Announces three-year survey of Muncie blacks by
          Virginia Commonwealth University professors Rutledge
          M. Dennis and Vivian V. Gordon. Research, to begin
          in summer, seeks to demonstrate importance of blacks
          to community, a neglected theme in Lynd and
          Middletown III studies.

368. Bahr, Howard M. "Changes in Family Life in
          Middletown, 1924-77." PUBLIC OPINION QUARTERLY 44
          (Spring 1980): 35-52.

          Compares 1924 and 1977 high school surveys, finding
          "generation gap" about the same, with alienation
          between parents and youth no greater than before.

369. Austin, Penelope Canan. "The Federal Presence in
          Middletown: 1937-1977." THE TOCQUEVILLE REVIEW 2
          (Spring-Summer 1980): 93-107.

          Describes proliferation of federal programs in
          Middletown since 1930s, arguing that Lynds'
          prediction of "blurring of local administrative
          autonomy" clearly has been realized. Notes present
          research has focused on executive branch of
          government, but also should look at impact of
          judicial branch.

1980

370.   Frankland, E. Gene, Michael Corbett, and Dorothy
        Rudoni. "Value Priorities of College Students."
        YOUTH AND SOCIETY 11 (March 1980): 267-93.

        Analyzes results of Ball State University student
        survey, noting that more than 90% came from
        "Middletown" and surrounding environs. Also draws
        comparisons to preliminary Middletown III findings.

371.   Caplow, Theodore, and Margaret Holmes Williamson.
        "Decoding Middletown's Easter Bunny: A Study in
        American Iconography." SEMIOTICA 32 (March/April
        1980): 221-32.

        Explores the symbolism behind Middletown holidays,
        both secular and religious, and ways holidays are
        represented and celebrated.

372.   Guterbock, Thomas M. "Social Class and Voting
        Choices in Middletown." SOCIAL FORCES 58 (June
        1980): 1044-56.

        Analyzes voting patterns, arguing that class voting
        in Middletown persists despite general decrease of
        class differences.

373.   Geelhoed, Bruce E. "Business and the American
        Family: A Local View." INDIANA SOCIAL STUDIES
        QUARTERLY 33 (Autumn 1980): 58-67.

        Argues that success factors of small businesses in
        social laboratory known as Middletown include strong
        family involvement, exceptional adaptability, and
        high degree of community involvement.

374.   Lynd, Helen Merrell. "Middletown." American
        Sociological Association COMMUNITY SECTION
        NEWSLETTER, 10 (Fall 1980): 1-5.

        Transcript of speech given in acceptance of Second
        Annual Community Section Award. Describes
        experiences in Muncie while collecting data for
        first Middletown Study.

1980

375.   Vander Hill, C. Warren. "Middletown: The Most
        Studied Community in America." INDIANA SOCIAL
        STUDIES QUARTERLY 33 (Autumn 1980): 47-57.

        Revised version of essay in MIDDLETOWN MAN (see
        item 231), describing Lynds' methodology, community
        changes since Lynd studies, and recent findings of
        Middletown III researchers.

376.   Hadden, Jeffrey K. "H. Paul Douglass: His
        Perspective and His Work." REVIEW OF RELIGIOUS
        RESEARCH 22 (September 1980): 66-88.

        Includes examination of Douglass' association with
        Institute for Social and Religious Research, which
        funded Lynds' first study.

377.   Geary, Katie. "Japanese to Film Life in
        Middletown, U.S.A." MUNCIE STAR, 8 October 1980,
        p. 20.

        Announces arrival of film crews for Japanese
        documentary on American life, one segment dealing
        with "average American family" in Muncie.

378.   "Middletown Study Reports Family Is Healthy as Ever."
        MUNCIE EVENING PRESS, 11 October 1980, p. 1.

        Caplow shares findings of Middletown III study,
        showing that American family is alive and well
        despite rumors of decline. Significant rise,
        however, in number of female heads of households
        since Lynd studies.

379.   "Family Demise Exaggerated, 'Middletown' Sociologist
        Says." MUNCIE STAR, 12 October 1980, sec. A, p. 1.

        UPI story notes Caplow's Middletown III findings
        about thriving American family, as described in
        forthcoming book.

1980

380.   Friedman, Saul. "Touring Newsman Finds Muncie
        'Apathetic' to Election." MUNCIE STAR, 15 October
        1980, p. 4.

        Knight-Ridder story, reporting from Pittsburgh,
        Buffalo and Muncie, whether neither Democrats nor
        Republicans enthusiastic about presidential race.

381.   "Muncie Atypical?" MUNCIE STAR, 20 October 1980,
        p. 4.

        Editorial criticizes myths about declining American
        family, citing findings from Middletown III.

382.   "Muncie Family Subject of Japanese TV Film." MUNCIE
        STAR, 21 October 1980, p. 11.

        Notes that Japanese Fuji network filming documentary
        on "typical" American family. Middletown film
        series crew also in town, shooting the Fuji crew
        shooting the Evans family.

383.   Davis, Jim. "Garfield." MUNCIE STAR, 11 November 1980,
        p. 17.

        Guest appearance in popular cartoon by Garfield's
        grandfather, noted as "best ratter in Middletown."

384.   Bump, Dorothea. "Crime in 'Good Old Days' Higher
        Than Today, BSU Study Indicates." MUNCIE STAR, 16
        November 1980, sec. A, p. 10.

        Discusses research of Ball State professor John
        Hewitt on criminal cases in Middletown from 1820 to
        1900. Notes that crime in many cases is similar.

385.   "Latest Findings in Middletown Study to be Unveiled."
        MUNCIE STAR, 16 November 1980, sec. A, p. 1.

        Announces forthcoming lecture by Theodore Caplow, 18
        November 1980, on Middletown III findings. Also
        gives background on Middletown III researchers and
        Center for Middletown Studies.

1980

386.   Hawes, G.K. "Middletown May Be Typical After
        All, Says Researcher." MUNCIE STAR, 18 November
        1980, p. 1.

        Discusses Center for Middletown Studies dedication
        lecture by Theodore Caplow, who notes that Muncie
        not exactly typical but does tend to fall around the
        median on most sociological measures. Also cites
        numerous studies of Muncie since Lynds.

387.   LaGuardia, Joan D. "Middletown Study Reveals
        Myth of Declining Family." MUNCIE EVENING PRESS, 18
        November 1980, pp. 1, 2.

        Middletown III researcher Caplow, at lecture in
        Muncie, describes resilience of the family and notes
        two new areas of study: influence of television and
        impact of federal government presence. Black
        Middletown study also discussed.

388.   Atteberry, Mary Wade. "Latest 'Middletown' Study
        Reveals Muncie Still Has Its Magic Quality."
        INDIANAPOLIS STAR, 19 November 1980, p. 18.

        Reports comments by Caplow on continuity of
        Middletown families and research techniques employed
        by Middletown III project, replicating Lynd studies
        and addressing new issues such as impact of
        television and federal government.

389.   Hawes, G.K. "Family, Work Ethic Surviving in Muncie."
        MUNCIE STAR, 19 November 1980, pp. 1, 8.

        Reports on lecture by Caplow, who notes that myth of
        family decline can be traced to committee
        commissioned by President Hoover in late 1920s.
        Also discusses other Middletown findings.

1980

390.   "No decline in Work Ethic Seen in Middletown."
        BLOOMINGTON HERALD TELEPHONE, 19 November 1980,
        p. 29.

        UPI story on Middletown III findings reported by
        Theodore Caplow. Notes that decline of work ethic,
        like family decline, largely myth. Story carried by
        numerous other Indiana newspapers.

391.   "Study Shows Muncie Still Typical 'Middletown'
        USA." ANDERSON (Ind.) DAILY BULLETIN, 19 November
        1980, p. 14.

        AP story on Middletown III researcher, Theodore
        Caplow, speech for opening of Center for Middletown
        Studies at Ball State. Notes persistence of family
        values, but other changes in areas of leisure
        activities and impact of federal programs. Separate
        study of black Middletown residents forthcoming.
        Story carried by numerous other Indiana newspapers.

392.   "Who Says the 'Good Ol' Days' Were Better?" FORT WAYNE
        (Ind.) NEWS-SENTINEL, 20 November 1980, sec. C,
        p. 24.

        UPI story, taken from Bump article (see item 384),
        reports on John Hewitt's findings regarding crime in
        Middletown. Story carried by numerous Indiana
        newspapers and elsewhere, including HOUSTON
        CHRONICLE.

393.   Hawes, G.K. "Here's a Look at Slumping Auto Industry."
        MUNCIE STAR, 20 November 1980, pp. 1, 6.

        Discusses program "Reflections of a Giant: The
        Indiana Automotive Industry in Retrospect" with
        moderator, Ball State Professor Vander Hill,
        reflecting upon Lynds' critique of automobile's
        impact on American society.

1980

394.   Stodghill, Dick.   "In the Press of Things."   MUNCIE
       EVENING PRESS, 26 November 1980, p. 2.

       Resents Muncie tag as typical or commonplace and
       goes on to cite examples, both good and bad, which
       are not representative of average community.

395.   Graff, Don.   "Middletown (Muncie) Is Law-Abiding."
       ANDERSON (Indiana) BULLETIN, 29 November 1980.

       Newspaper Enterprise Association story, somewhat
       shorter than UPI version, on Hewitt's crime report.
       Carried by several other Indiana newspapers.

396.   Burgchardt, Carl.   "Two Faces of American Communism:
       Pamphlet Rhetoric of the Third Period and the
       Popular Front."   QUARTERLY JOURNAL OF SPEECH, 66
       (December 1980): 375-91.

       Includes discussion of Middletown's reaction to
       1930s communist propaganda.   Predominant attitude
       that communists trying to "wreck American
       civilization."

397.   Kasen, Jill H.   "Whither the Self-made Man?
       Comic Culture and the Crisis of Legitimation in the
       United States."   SOCIAL PROBLEMS 28 (December 1980):
       131-48.

       Notes time lag between business oriented/industrial
       reality of 1920s, as depicted by Lynds, and comic
       culture which still looked back to an earlier
       pastoral ideal.

398.   Rossi, Peter H.   "The Presidential Address: The
       Challenge and Opportunities of Applied Research."
       AMERICAN SOCIOLOGICAL REVIEW 45 (December 1980):
       889-904.

       Cites Lynds' initial study as early example of
       qualitative research methods, funded by foundation
       concerned with "impact of social change on the moral
       life of Americans."

1980

399.   "Album of Yesteryear." MUNCIE STAR, 2 December
        1980, sec. C, p. 9.

        Photograph of federal housing homes (Lynds'
        "Shedtown") in Muncie.

400.   "NBC Planning Another Look at 'Middletown.'"
        MUNCIE STAR, 11 December 1980, p. 3.

        Announces NBC film crew, with Fred Briggs, to be in
        Muncie during January 1981. Interviews planned with
        residents who were part of original Middletown study
        and director of Middletown III project, Theodore
        Caplow.

1981

401.   Caplow, Theodore. "Evaluation des changements
        sociaux a Middletown." In SCIENCE ET THEORIE DE
        L'OPINION PUBLIQUE, edited by R. Boudon, F.
        Bourricaud, and A.A. Girard, 49-60. Paris: Retz,
        1981.

        French translation, slightly revised, of "Half a
        Century of Change..." (see item 314).

402.   Lynd, Robert Staughton. THE PAPERS OF ROBERT AND
        HELEN MERRELL LYND, 1895-1968. Washington, D.C.:
        Library of Congress Photoduplication Service, 1981.

        Contains microfilm copies of correspondence,
        research materials, writings and lectures, primarily
        from period 1922-1960. Much of collection, held by
        Library of Congress, pertains to Middletown studies.

1981

403.   Ray, Scott.   "The Depressed Industrial Society:
        Occupational Movement, Out-Migration and Residential
        Mobility in the Industrial-Urbanization of
        Middletown, 1880-1925."   Ph.D. diss., Ball State
        University, 1981.

        Challenges Lynds' blocked-mobility thesis, arguing
        that social mobility decreased during period under
        study, but in conjunction with deceleration rather
        than advent of industrialization.

404.   Walker, David B.   "Signs of the System's Overload."   In
        TOWARD A FUNCTIONING FEDERALISM, edited by David B.
        Walker, 3-16.   Cambridge, Mass.: Winthrop
        Publishers, 1981.

        Examines effects of federal aid in Muncie as example
        of increasingly intrusive nature of federal
        presence.

405.   Caplow, Theodore, Howard M. Bahr, and Bruce A. Chadwick.
        "Piety in Middletown."   SOCIETY 18 (January/February
        1981): 34-37.

        Argues that strength of religion in Middletown not
        due to flight from other failed social institutions.
        Suggests, instead, a Tocquevillean explanation that
        religion, rather than government or local community,
        in a democratic and egalitarian society, best can
        provide moral authority that acts as behavioral
        constraint on individuals.

406.   Kluegel, James R., and Eliot R. Smith.   "Beliefs
        About Stratification."   ANNUAL REVIEW OF SOCIOLOGY 7
        (1981): 29-56.

        Includes discussion of role of "class" and "class
        consciousness" in examination of stratification
        beliefs, arguing that early studies like Lynds'
        often oversimplified.

1981

407.   Langford, Scott. "'Middletown' Muncie Studied."
        BALL STATE DAILY NEWS, 6 January 1981, p. 1.

        Announces that NBC film crew to be in Muncie to film
        another segment for "Today" show. Gives history and
        importance of Middletown studies.

408.   "NBC Muncie Broadcast Delayed." BALL STATE DAILY
        NEWS, 20 January 1981, p. 2.

        NBC to delay filming of Muncie segment for "Today"
        show, primarily because Caplow unavailable for
        interview.

409.   Caplow, Theodore, Howard M. Bahr, and Bruce A.
        Chadwick. "Piety in Middletown." TRANSACTION
        MAGAZINE 18 (January/February 1981): 34-37.

        Comparison of several 1977-78 surveys with earlier
        Lynd findings. Shows dramatic increase in church
        buildings and attendance, greater financial support,
        disappearance of class differences regarding
        religious favor, and a markedly higher degree of
        religious tolerance.

410.   Rossi, Peter H. "Postwar Applied Social Research:
        Growth and Opportunities." AMERICAN BEHAVIORAL
        SCIENTIST 24 (January/February 1981): 445-61.

        Slightly edited version of Presidential Address (see
        item 398).

411.   Hawes, G.K. "Researchers to Start Monday on Black
        Muncie Survey." MUNCIE STAR 1 February 1981, p. 1.

        Describes of upcoming Black Middletown Study, which
        will include oral history and survey techniques.

1981

412. Wilcox, Sue Ellen. "Muncie's Family, Home Life
      Are Not Unstable, Expert Says." MUNCIE EVENING
      PRESS, 4 February 1981, p. 1.

      Ball State home economics professor and marriage
      counselor, Richard Carr, cites communication and
      financial difficulties as major marriage problems,
      but agrees with Middletown III findings that decline
      of family is myth in Muncie.

413. "'Today' Interviews City Residents." BALL STATE
      DAILY NEWS, 5 February 1981, p. 2.

      Announces arrival of NBC film crew to do segment for
      "Today" show. Caplow, director of Middletown III
      project, acting as advisor to NBC.

414. Langford, Scott. "'Today' Reports on Middletown." BALL
      STATE DAILY NEWS, 11 February 1981, p. 3.

      Interviews NBC correspondent Fred Briggs about
      Middletown segment for "Today" show. Notes that no
      definite air date set (not shown).

415. McPherson, J. Miller. "Dynamic Model of Voluntary
      Affiliation." SOCIAL FORCES 59 (March 1981):
      705-28.

      Includes discussion of Lynds' work and other early
      community studies that found strong correlation
      between socioeconomic status and rate of joining
      voluntary associations.

416. Langford, Scott. "'Black Middletown' Project
      Receives Attention: Study Begins." BALL STATE DAILY
      NEWS, 13 March 1981, p. 5.

      Discusses preliminary findings of Black Middletown
      Study, co-directed by Rutledge Dennis and Vivian
      Gordon, and describes use of surveys and oral
      history as research techniques. Notes failure of
      Lynds and Middletown III replication study to
      investigate condition of blacks in Middletown.

1981

417.   Langford, Scott. "Center Receives Money: Orders
        Tape Recorders." BALL STATE DAILY NEWS, 18 March
        1981, p. 3.

        Reports that Center for Middletown Studies to
        receive equipment to augment historical record of
        Middletown, through collection of oral histories and
        historical photographs.

418.   Lingeman, Richard. "Hanging Together in Muncie,
        Ind." Psychology Today 14 (May 1981): 8-13.

        Summarizes findings of forthcoming MIDDLETOWN
        FAMILIES (see item 438), most surprising being
        conclusion that Middletown and its families have not
        changed substantially in last five decades. Sees
        retention of traditional institutions as defensive
        reaction against modern society that is not fully
        understood.

419.   Lingeman, Richard. "The Family Is Alive and Well
        in Muncie." CHICAGO TRIBUNE, 3 May 1981, sec. 2,
        pp. 1, 4.

        Outlines major findings in forthcoming MIDDLETOWN
        FAMILIES, reflecting upon strength of nuclear family
        and associated kinship ties as reaction to "a
        society that has become increasingly remote,
        impersonal, bureaucratized, and threatening."

420.   Amiot, Michel. "Au Middle West rein de nouveau."
        LE MONDE DIMANCHIE, 10 May 1981, pp. 11, 14.

        Interviews Caplow, who describes background of
        Middletown studies and latest findings which
        indicate surprising lack of change.

1981

421. Titus, A. Constandina. "Local Governmental
       Expenditures and Political Attitudes: A Look at Nine
       Major Cities." URBAN AFFAIRS QUARTERLY 16 (June
       1981): 437-52.

       Includes review of the literature, referring to
       initial Lynd study as early example of trend toward
       community power studies which lasted until 1960s.

422. Lobsenz, Norman. "News from the Home Front. The
       Family: Holding Firm." FAMILY WEEKLY, 2 August 1981,
       p. 9.

       Brief synopsis of findings from MIDDLETOWN FAMILIES.

423. Yager, Florence. "BSU Student Says Lynds Missed
       Mark on 'Middletown' Studies." MUNCIE STAR,
       9 August 1981, sec. D, p. 12.

       Xavier University professor Scott Ray, in a recently
       completed Ball State dissertation (see item 403)
       argues that upward mobility in 1920s Muncie was
       limited less by industrialization, as Lynds
       contended, than end of gas boom.

424. "Revisiting Middletown: 50 Years Later, the American
       Family Is Alive and Well in Muncie, Indiana."
       PEOPLE, 17 August 1981, 24-27.

       Preview of MIDDLETOWN FAMILIES findings,
       supplemented by interviews of local residents.
       Discussion focuses on stable marriage rates, equal
       sex roles, extended families and Midwest work ethic.

425. Caplow, Theodore. "The Sociological Myth of
       Family Decline." TOCQUEVILLE REVIEW 3 (Fall 1981):
       349-69.

       Describes changes from 1920s to 1970s, including
       "increased family solidarity, a smaller generation
       gap, closer marital communication, more religion,
       and less mobility." Suggests myth of family decline
       psychologically useful to individuals when comparing
       own situation to supposedly deteriorated norm.

1981

426.   North, Juli, and Katy Geary. "Rockefeller-Lynd
        Connection Told: Led to Middletown Studies." MUNCIE
        STAR, 13 September 1981, sec. C, p. 1.

        Discusses talk by Charles Harvey about the Institute
        of Social Religious Research, an agency financed by
        John D. Rockefeller, Jr., which sponsored Lynds'
        initial Middletown research.

427.   Stone, Judy. Review of "The Campaign." SAN FRANCISCO
        CHRONICLE, 10 October 1981, p. 23.

        Views first segment of Peter Davis' Middletown film
        series at Palace of Fine Arts and finds it
        compelling human drama, but faults it for failing to
        examine role of local power structure in determining
        outcome of mayoral election depicted.

428.   Ferguson, Jon. "Local Professors to Speak: Baltimore to
        Host Religious Symposium." BALL STATE DAILY NEWS,
        30 October 1981, p. 1.

        Professors Dwight Hoover and Joseph Tamney outline
        upcoming papers for meeting of the Society for the
        Scientific Study of Religion. Emphasis on
        historical aspects of religion in Middletown.

429.   Stone, Judy. "Elections, Middletown Style:
        Documentary Shows Elections as 'Human Drama.'"
        MUNCIE WEEKLY NEWS, 5 November 1981, p. 5.

        Reprint of article in SAN FRANCISCO CHRONICLE (see
        item 427).

1982

430.   THE CAMPAIGN. Middletown Film Series no. 1.
        Pittsburgh, Pa.: WQED/PBS-TV, 1982.

        Uses cinema verite approach in tracing 1980 Muncie
        mayoral race between Republican Alan Wilson and
        Democrat James Carey. Corresponds with Lynd's
        "Participating in Community Activities" section.   90
        minute segment first aired 24 March 1982.

431.   THE BIG GAME. Middletown Film Series no. 3.
        Pittsburgh, Pa.: WQED/PBS-TV, 1982.

        Traces basketball rivalry between Muncie Central's
        Bearcats and Anderson's Indians. Corresponds with
        Lynds' "Using Leisure" section. 60 Minute segment
        first aired 31 March 1982.

432.   A COMMUNITY OF PRAISE. Middletown Film Series
        no. 2. Pittsburgh, Pa.: WQED/PBS-TV, 1982.

        Investigates one of a growing number of charismatic
        religious cults based in Muncie area. Corresponds
        with Lynds' "Engaging in Religious Practices"
        section. 60 minute segment first aired 7 April
        1982.

433.   FAMILY BUSINESS. Middletown Film Series no. 4.
        Pittsburgh, Pa.: WQED/PBS-TV, 1982.

        Examines Snider family's problems as they attempt to
        save its faltering Shakey's pizza franchise.
        Corresponds with Lynds' "Getting a Living" section.
        90 minute segment first aired 14 April 1982.

434.   SECOND TIME AROUND. Middletown Film Series
        no. 5. Pittsburgh, Pa.: WQED/PBS-TV, 1982.

        Follows David Shesler and Elaine Ingram, both
        divorced, as they court and plan to marry.
        Corresponds with Lynds' "Making a Home" section.
        60 minute segment first aired 21 April 1982.

1982

435.   MIDDLETOWN REVISITED: WITH BEN WATTENBERG.
        Muncie, Ind.: WIPB/PBS-TV, 1982.

        Last segment of series, produced by local PBS
        affiliate WIPB-TV and hosted by Ben Wattenberg.
        Replacement for "Seventeen" segment, which was
        withdrawn by Producer Davis. 60 minute segment,
        first aired 28 April 1982.

436.   Caplow, Theodore. LOOKING FOR SECULARIZATION IN
        MIDDLETOWN. Talk given at annual meeting of Friends
        of Alexander M. Bracken Library, 27 April 1982.
        Muncie, Ind.: Ball State University, Friends of
        Bracken Library, 1982.

        Contends that Middletown III data shows continued
        resilience of religion in Muncie, although
        admittedly puzzled why this should be case in
        America and not other advanced industrial nations.

437.   Caplow, Theodore. "La Repetition de enquetes: une
        methode de recherche sociologique." L'ANNEE
        SOCIOLOGIQUE 32 (1982): 9-22.

        Describes Middletown III replication of Lynd
        studies, and suggests typology for various
        sociological restudies.

438.   Caplow, Theodore, et al. MIDDLETOWN FAMILIES:
        FIFTY YEARS OF CHANGE AND CONTINUITY. Minneapolis:
        University of Minnesota Press, 1982.

        First of several projected volumes analyzing
        Middletown III data. Individual chapters by
        Theodore Caplow, Howard M. Bahr, Bruce A. Chadwick,
        Reuben Hill and Margaret Holmes Williamson. Central
        thesis that family alive and well in Muncie, and
        less changed than anticipated.

1982

439.   Cunningham, Bob. GROWING UP IN MIDDLETOWN,
        U.S.A. Vols. 1-5. Muncie, Ind.: Privately printed,
        1982-1987.

        Collection of personal reminiscences and drawings,
        first appearing in MUNCIE EVENING PRESS.

440.   Davis, Peter. HOMETOWN. New York: Simon and
        Schuster, 1982.

        Offers intimate portrayal of Hamilton, Ohio, using
        Lynds' social research categories of work, play,
        education, religion, family and politics. Some
        chapters, such as "The Wedding" and "The Game"
        strongly reminiscent of episodes from Middletown
        film series.

441.   Geelhoed, E. Bruce. BRINGING WALL STREET TO MAIN
        STREET: THE STORY OF K.J. BROWN & COMPANY, INC.,
        1931-1981. Ball State University Business History
        Series, No. 1. Muncie, Ind.: Ball State University,
        1982.

        Traces rise of Muncie-based brokerage firm.
        Occasional Middletown references, particularly in
        chapter 1: "Middletown's Broker."

442.   Hewit, John Scott. "A Study of Preschool Child
        Care in Middletown USA." Ed.D. thesis, Ball State
        University, 1982.

        Argues that demands on working parents have led to
        more non-parental care than recognized in previous
        Middletown research.

1982

443.   Kirchner, Jack M. "The Insane: A Study of Their
        Diagnosis and Subsequent Treatment from Ancient to
        Modern Times, with a Focus on Indiana, and a Case
        Study of Delaware County from 1869 to 1927." Ph.D.
        diss., Ball State University, 1982.

        Chapter on Delaware County includes discussion of
        Lynds' research on changes in state care,
        particularly as evidenced by county poor asylum,
        during 1890-1920s period.

444.   Lingeman, Richard. "The Campaign." In MIDDLETOWN
        TEACHING NOTES. New York: Learning Designs and The
        Middletown Film Project, 1982.

        Guide to Middletown film series segment "The
        Campaign," which follows 1979 Muncie mayoral race
        between two candidates with widely differing styles
        and backgrounds.

445.   McQuade, Donald. "Community of Praise." In
        MIDDLETOWN TEACHING NOTES. New York: Learning
        Designs and The Middletown Film Project, 1982.

        Guide to Middletown film series segment "Community
        of Praise," which documents lives and beliefs of an
        evangelical Christian family.

446.   Trachtenberg, Alan. "Family Business." In
        MIDDLETOWN TEACHING NOTES. New York: Learning
        Designs and The Middletown Film Project, 1982.

        Guide to Middletown film series segment "Family
        Business," which depicts struggle to save a pizza
        parlor franchise in financial straits.

447.   Trillan, Alice. "Second Time Around." In
        MIDDLETOWN TEACHING NOTES. New York: Learning
        Design and The Middletown Film Project, 1982.

        Guide to Middletown film series segment "Second Time
        Around," which follows relationship and wedding
        plans of a couple, both previously married.

1982

448.   Trillan, Alice, and Joseph F. Trimmer. MIDDLETOWN
        TEACHING NOTES. New York: Learning Designs and The
        Middletown Film Project, 1982.

        Guide to Middletown film series, with critical
        analysis of each segment, pre- and post-viewing
        questions, and suggested readings.

449.   Trimmer, Joseph F. "The Big Game." In MIDDLETOWN
        TEACHING NOTES. New York: Learning Designs and
        The Middletown Film Project, 1982.

        Guide to Middletown film series segment "The Big
        Game," which traces preparations and meeting of
        longtime basketball rivals, Muncie Central and
        Anderson high schools.

450.   Trimmer, Joseph F. "Seventeen." IN MIDDLETOWN
        TEACHING NOTES. New York: Learning Designs and The
        Middletown Film Project, 1982.

        Guide to Middletown film series segment "Seventeen,"
        which traces lives of a group of high school
        seniors. Not aired.

451.   Hewitt, John D., and Dwight W. Hoover. "Local
        Modernization and Crime: The Effects of
        Modernization and Crime in Middletown, 1845-1910."
        LAW AND HUMAN BEHAVIOR 6, 3/4 (1982): 313-25.

        Investigates impact of industrialization and
        urbanization on criminal behavior during period of
        Muncie's greatest growth.

452.   "About 'Middletown.'" HEADLINES (Quarterly
        Newsletter of the Indiana Committee for the
        Humanities), Winter 1982, pp. 3-4.

        Provides overview of Middletown studies and
        summarizes content of each "Middletown" film
        segment. Includes suggestions for educational
        applications.

1982

453.   "The 'Middletown' Series: Indiana Background."
        HEADLINES (Quarterly Newsletter of the Indiana
        Committee for the Humanities), Winter 1982, p. 3.

        Summarizes financial role of Indiana Committee for
        the Humanities in planning and production of
        Middletown film series.

454.   Ratier-Coutrot, Laurence. "Le Programme de
        recherche sur Middletown III." SOCIOLOGIE DU
        TRAVAIL 24 (January-March 1982): 95-102.

        Summarizes and critiques individual surveys
        conducted by Middletown III Project. Includes
        discussion of Black Middletown Project.

455.   Stodghill, Dick. "Book Writer Made It Clear;
        Muncie Didn't Impress Him." MUNCIE EVENING PRESS,
        20 January 1982, p. 2.

        Belated review of DRIVEN (see item 266), noting
        Mandel's indictment of automotive-oriented American
        society.

456.   Cannon, Harold. "Helen Lynd on Middletown." HUMANITIES
        (National Endowment for the Humanities) 3 (February
        1982): 2.

        Notes from Lynd's memoirs, POSSIBILITIES, describing
        how the study of Middletown was initiated, staffed,
        financed and published.

457.   Leigh, Geoffrey K. "Kinship Interaction over
        the Family Life Span." JOURNAL OF MARRIAGE AND THE
        FAMILY 44 (February 1982): 197-208.

        From dissertation of same title (see item 307).

1982

458.   Wolfson, Barbara Delman. "Middletown: Plus ça change."
        HUMANITIES (National Endowment for the Humanities),
        3 (February 1982): 3-5.

        Previews Middletown film series, also discussing
        other studies that have looked to Muncie as
        "barometer of national attitudes." Traces evolution
        of series and Davis' approach of searching for drama
        in ordinary situations.

459.   "Helen Lynd, MIDDLETOWN Co-Author, Dies at 85." MUNCIE
        EVENING PRESS, 1 February 1982, pp. 1, 10.

        From New York Times News Service, item 461.

460.   Chira, Susan. "Helen Merrell Lynd is Dead at 85;
        She, Husband Studied 'Middletown.'" MUNCIE STAR,
        1 February 1982, pp. 1, 6.

        From New York Times News Service, item 461.

461.   Chira, Susan. "Helen M. Lynd Dies; Co-author of
        'Middletown.'" NEW YORK TIMES, 1 February 1982,
        sec. B, p. 4.

        Obituary, with details about Lynd's Middletown work
        as well as other accomplishments, including ongoing
        concern with educational reform and social
        philosophy.

462.   Peterson, Iver. "In a 'Typical' U.S. Town,
        Revolutions Come Slowly: 50 Years After Sociologists
        Re-examine Values and Habits of a Small City." NEW
        YORK TIMES, 7 February 1982, sec. 4, p. 19.

        Summarizes Middletown III findings, noting that
        Muncie may be representative of Midwest, but
        debatable if more than that. Also argues that
        change in last 50 years not dramatic because Muncie
        already had developed from agrarian past to an
        industrial center by the time Lynds studied it.

1982

463.   Friedman, Saul. "Nation's Heartland Beginning to
        Show Fear of Depression." HARTFORD (Conn.) Courant,
        14 February 1982, sec. A, p. 16.

        Highlights Muncie citizens' fears of President
        Reagan's economic program. Discusses recession,
        unemployment, and business failures.

464.   Douglass, Joanne. "Uncovering Where the Spurgeons,
        Newtons and Other Families Thrive and Survive
        Despite 50 Years of Wars, Depression, Progress and
        Sociological Surveys." FRIENDLY EXCHANGE 2 (Spring
        1982): 28-32, 40.

        Traces history of Middletown studies and summarizes
        findings of forthcoming Middletown Families. Also
        interviews Spurgeon and Newton families, long-time
        residents of Muncie, about their perception of
        changes in Muncie and reaction to Middletown
        studies.

465.   Ohanlon, Timothy P. "School Sports as Social
        Training: The Case of Athletics and the Crisis of
        World War I." JOURNAL OF SPORT HISTORY 9 (Spring
        1982): 5-29.

        Cites Lynd studies in discussion of relationship of
        education to occupational roles and social class.

466.   Wirthlin, Laura. "The Middletown Film Series:
        Historians' Perspectives." JANUS (Newsletter for
        history majors and minors at Ball State University),
        Spring 1982, p. 1

        Traces development of Middletown Film Project and
        limited influence of historians upon final project.

1982

467.   Bahr, Howard M. "Youth and the Church in Middletown."
        TOCQUEVILLE REVIEW 4 (Spring-Summer 1982): 31-63.

        Findings based on data from Middletown III school
        survey, indicate persistence of dominant Christian
        beliefs, but greater tolerance for other viewpoints
        than in 1920s. Notes that gender and father's
        occupational class not significant variables for
        attitudes and beliefs.

468.   Bahr, Howard M. "The Perrigo Paper: A Local Influence
        upon Middletown in Transition." INDIANA MAGAZINE OF
        HISTORY 78 (March 1982): 1-25.

        Investigates Lynds' use of research paper by Muncie
        resident, Lynn I. Perrigo, most notably in
        Middletown in Transition chapter on X family.

469.   Elkin, Stanley. "How Average Are the Folks in
        'Middletown, U.S.A.'?" DIAL (March 1982): 13-17.

        Humorous cartoon approach to 1982 Middletown, with
        favorable critique of Davis' Middletown series.
        Chronological list of various past Middletown dates,
        including note on Muncie as setting for 1977 film
        "Close Encounters of the Third Kind."

470.   Emerson, Gloria. "TV Documentary of the Year: Middle
        America Revisited." VOGUE, March 1982, p. 64.

        Previews upcoming Middletown film series, noting
        effectiveness of close range camera in capturing
        "crucial periods in the lives of people not at all
        certain of success."

471.   Terhune, Bill. "New TV Documentary About Muncie
        Is a No-holds-barred Blockbuster." MUNCIE EVENING
        PRESS, 4 March 1982, pp. 1, 13.

        Attends preview of "The Campaign" and finds it
        engrossing. Describes several of episode's scenes.

1982

472.   LaGuardia, Joan D. "TV Series on Muncie Is too
        'Raw' for One Sponsor." MUNCIE EVENING PRESS, 9
        March 1982, pp. 1, 4.

        Local audience reacts adversely to preview of
        "Seventeen" segment of Middletown film series. Also
        notes that Xerox Corporation has withdrawn support
        for project and school officials examining
        agreements with filmmakers.

473.   Shores, Larry. "'Middletown', 6-Part Series on
        Muncie, Gets the Bad Word." MUNCIE STAR, 9 March
        1982, p. 1.

        Discusses content of "Seventeen" episode and local
        reaction that Davis wanted students to look bad.
        Notes Xerox Corporation's difficulty with segment,
        threatening to pull sponsorship if aired.

474.   LaGuardia, Joan D. "PBS Says 'Wait and See' as TV
        Controversy Grows." MUNCIE EVENING PRESS, 10 March
        1982, pp. 1, 6.

        Comments from PBS Programming representative, mother
        of student featured in "Seventeen" segment, and
        other Southside students.

475.   "Muncie to Take a Look at Those Looking at Us."
        MUNCIE EVENING PRESS, 10 March 1982, p. 6.

        Reports local PBS affiliate to produce program
        examining all segments of Middletown series.
        Currently negotiating for national host.

476.   North, Juli. "PBS 'Seventeen' Segment Fills
        Southsiders with Anger, Dismay." MUNCIE STAR, 12
        March 1982, pp. 1, 12.

        Gives local reaction to preview of "Seventeen,"
        including quotes by teachers, students, and
        principal of Muncie Southside High School.

1982

477.   "Xerox Pulls Out of 'Middletown' - Blames Profanity."
        TV GUIDE (Central Indiana Edition), 13 March 1982,
        sec. A, pp. 1, 5.

        Discusses decision of Xerox, who put up $600,000 for
        the series, to withdraw its sponsorship due to
        differences over content of "Seventeen."

478.   Ellsworth-Jones, Will. "Happy Families: America
        Is Full of Them, Says the Latest Message from
        Middletown, USA." SUNDAY TIMES (London), 14 March
        1982, sec. 1, p. 14.

        Critical analysis of Middletown III project, raising
        questions about supposed well-being of American
        family as viewed in Middletown.

479.   Hill, Doug. "Documentarian Focuses on Middle America."
        NEW YORK TIMES, 14 March 1982, sec. D, p. 25.

        Focuses on Davis as filmmaker, listing previous
        credits and details about Middletown Film Project.

480.   LaGuardia, Joan D. "Former Southside Girl Says
        Lens Turned Her, Others Into 'Hot Shots.'" MUNCIE
        EVENING PRESS, 15 March 1982, pp. 1, 6.

        Claims that students in "Seventeen" were playing to
        the camera and that classroom shots were not
        representative of education at Southside.

481.   Grieves, Carolyn. "Seventeen Damages South." MUNCIE
        EVENING PRESS, 16 March 1982, p. 5.

        Open letter from Southside teacher, to James
        Needham, manager of local PBS affiliate WIPB
        criticizing him for negative content of "Seventeen"
        episode.

1982

482.   Terhune, Bill. "The Seamier Side: PBS Film's Sin Lies
        in Avoiding Dullness." MUNCIE EVENING PRESS, 16
        March 1982, p. 4.

        Notes that "Seventeen's" depiction of Southside
        students may be one-sided, but holds interest of
        audience. Three segments of series previewed
        locally to date.

483.   Wilson, Scott. "Real Education." MUNCIE STAR, 16 March
        1982, p. 3,

        Letter to editor from Muncie Southside student,
        stating that incidents depicted in "Seventeen"
        episode of Middletown series could have taken place
        at any local high school.

484.   "An Apology to James Needham." MUNCIE EVENING PRESS,
        17 March 1982, p. 7.

        EVENING PRESS apologizes for Grieves' letter (see
        item 481) which erroneously implied that Needham was
        responsible for content of Middletown series.

485.   Coughlin, Ellen K. "'Middletown' Much the Same
        After 50 Years, Study Finds, but Sociology Greatly
        Changed." CHRONICLE OF HIGHER EDUCATION, 17 March
        1982, pp. 19-20.

        Review of Middletown Families, summarizing findings
        and noting shift to quantitative and analytical
        techniques in social sciences.

486.   LaGuardia, Joan D. "School Delegation Flies to
        PBS Parley." MUNCIE EVENING PRESS, 17 March 1982,
        p. 1.

        Notes that Muncie School superintendent, manager of
        WIPB, and others to present PBS officials with
        information, reportedly including student statements
        to school attorney.

1982

487.   North, Juli. "PBS's 'Seventeen' Inspires Trip."
        MUNCIE STAR, 17 March 1982, p. 1.

        Notice that Muncie delegation traveling to
        Washington to meet with PBS officials about
        Seventeen' although specific agenda for meeting not
        disclosed.

488.   Hawes, G.K. "'Seventeen' Delegation Has Nothing to
        Report." MUNCIE STAR, 18 March 1982, p. 5.

        Notes that Muncie delegation not prepared to talk
        about results of meeting with PBS officials.

489.   LaGuardia, Joan D. "Middletown Subject Likes His
        Experience." MUNCIE EVENING PRESS, 18 March 1982,
        pp. 1, 14.

        Howard Snider describes his experiences making the
        "Family Business" segment of "Middletown" series.

490.   Lehmann-Haupt, Christopher. "Books of the Times." NEW
        YORK TIMES, 18 March 1982, sec. C, p. 24.

        Review of Davis' HOMETOWN (see item 440), noting
        intriguing prevalence of allegorical names such as a
        politician named Hack and a local contractor called
        Plasterer. Finds Davis' approach more a series of
        individual dramas than a community portrait, as done
        by Lynds with MIDDLETOWN.

491.   Hawes, G.K. "Legal Questions Studied by PBS." MUNCIE
        STAR, 19 March 1982, pp. 1, 7.

        Interviews WIPB manager James Needham, who suggests
        that local delegation presented PBS officials with
        information that may preclude airing of "Seventeen."

1982

492.   LaGuardia, Joan D.   "Some Southside Students Respond
       Editorially to PBS Program."   MUNCIE EVENING PRESS,
       19 March 1982, pp. 1, 6.

       Student newspaper editorial board suggests that
       "Seventeen" film crew may have encouraged and
       participated in many of activities shown in segment.

493.   Richey, Rodney.   "Producer of Documentary on Muncie
       Reacts to Reactions."   MUNCIE STAR, 19 March 1982,
       pp. 1, 7.

       Davis defends "Seventeen," arguing that it should
       not be viewed as statement on high schools in
       Muncie, but rather as view of 17-year-olds coming of
       age in Middle West.

494.   "Southside Students Mail Protests to PBS."   MUNCIE
       EVENING PRESS, 19 March 1982, p. 6.

       Excerpts letters criticizing "Seventeen."

495.   Baskin, John.   "Being Revealed Is a Bit Frightening."
       TV GUIDE (Central Indiana Edition), 20 March 1982,
       pp. 26-27, 29.

       Provides background on film series and examples of
       "intensely personal look" at lives of ordinary
       people in Middletown.

496.   Hawes, G.K.   "'Seventeen' Still on Schedule - for Now."
       MUNCIE STAR, 20 March 1982, p. 1.

       PBS officials state that "Seventeen" to be shown,
       although unspecified changes may be made.

497.   Jones, Sally.   "PBS Series on Muncie Premiers
       Wednesday."   MUNCIE EVENING PRESS, 20 March 1982,
       p. T-1.

       Summarizes upcoming segments and notes that each
       will be followed by local reaction program, shown
       only on WIPB.

1982

498.   "Middletown: The Campaign." TV GUIDE (Central Indiana
        edition), 20 March 1982, sec. A, p. 77.

        "Close-up" section features first segment of
        Middletown film series.

499.   Olinger, Mary Ann. "Controversial Look at Muncie
        Airs on PBS Beginning Wednesday." MUNCIE EVENING
        PRESS, 20 March 1982, p. T-2.

        Notes airing of part one of Middletown series on
        March 24, followed by local panel discussion.

500.   Shores, Larry. "An Untypical Television Show."
        MUNCIE STAR, 20 March 1982, sec. B, p. 8.

        Expresses concern about local reactions to
        "Seventeen" and bad light it shed on Muncie
        Southside High School. Suggests PBS plan
        introductory segment to provide perspective.

501.   Douglas, Donna. "Middletown: Seventeen." MUNCIE STAR,
        21 March 1982, sec. D, pp. 1, 2.

        Southside alumnus reviews unedited version of
        segment, after local showing, finding it boring,
        offensive, and lacking balance. Notes many things
        depicted also were taking place ten years earlier,
        during own high school days.

502.   Hermansen, Vicki. "Middletown: Family Business."
        MUNCIE STAR, 21 March 1982, sec. D, pp. 1, 2.

        Interview with Snider family, interspersed with
        information from segment. Describes family's
        feelings toward film crew and overall experience.

503.   Lough, Larry. "Middletown: The Campaign." MUNCIE STAR,
        21 March 1982, sec. D, pp. 1, 2.

        Reviews first segment of Middletown series, noting
        that Carey seemed more charming than Wilson, though
        still "full of baloney."

1982

504.   Shores, Larry. "Middletown: An Overview." MUNCIE STAR,
        21 March 1982, sec. D, pp. 1, 2.

        Reflects upon beginnings of Middletown Film Project,
        explaining why Muncie was chosen by Davis.

505.   Mitchell, Donald O. "Seventeen." MUNCIE STAR, 22 March
        1982, p. 4.

        Letter to editor, decrying efforts of local
        officials to censor "Seventeen" segment of
        Middletown series, and suggesting that Middletown
        citizenry intelligent enough to judge merits of
        segment for themselves.

506.   Unger, Arthur. "The People of 'Middletown' Decades
        Later: Is This a True Picture?" Christian Science
        Monitor, 23 March 1982, p. 19.

        Review of Middletown film series, noting its lack of
        balance and finding it "basically exploitive
        entertainment masquerading as a sociological
        document."

507.   LaGuardia, Joan D. "Mayor Finally Sees 'That' Film;
        WIPB to Show Two Versions." MUNCIE EVENING PRESS,
        24 March 1982, pp. 1, 6.

        Account of Alan Wilson's reaction to Middletown
        series first segment, "The Campaign."

508.   Miller, Casey. "'Middletown' Film Causes Controversy in
        Muncie." BALL STATE DAILY NEWS, 24 March 1982,
        p. 1.

        Provides update on local officials' protest of
        "Seventeen" showing on PBS.

1982

509.   Miller, Casey. "Middletown Debuts on Television."
         BALL STATE DAILY NEWS, 24 March 1982, p. 3.

         Explores history of Middletown studies and chain of
         events leading to PBS series. Summarizes first
         episode, "The Campaign."

510.   O'Connor John J. "TV: 'Middletown' in Video Verite."
         NEW YORK TIMES, 24 March 1982, sec. C, p. 23.

         Traces development of Middletown film series and
         finds it "brimming with shrewd insights and
         unsettling observations."

511.   Rosenberg, Howard. "Reality TV from Middle America."
         LOS ANGELES TIMES, 24 March 1982, sec. 6, pp. 1, 9.

         Review of Middletown series, focusing on "The
         Campaign" and finding it compelling.

512.   Shales, Tom. "TV's Stirring Vigil At the Crossroads."
         WASHINGTON POST, 24 March 1982, Sec. B, pp. 1, 15.

         Finds Middletown film series a significant
         accomplishment, proving that documentary form is not
         dead. Focuses primarily on "The Campaign" and
         "Seventeen."

513.   "Blame." MUNCIE STAR, 25 March 1982, p. 4.

         Letter to editor, arguing that Muncie Southside
         students who feel defensive about negative
         portrayals in "Seventeen," even though they don't
         share attitudes of segment's stars, should now
         understand how many law-abiding blacks feel when
         blamed for actions of the few.

1982

514.   Hawes, G.K. "PBS Offers Cleaned-Up 'Middletown'
        Program." MUNCIE STAR, 25 March 1982, pp. 1, 5.

        Explains how PBS used both edited and unedited
        versions of "The Campaign," offering affiliate
        stations choice. PBS also dropped promotional
        filler and article speculates why.

515.   Lough, Larry. "'Campaign' Rerun Plans Announced."
        MUNCIE STAR, 25 March 1982, p. 1, 5.

        Republican Alan Wilson and Democrat Jim Carey enter
        mayoral race and reflect upon impact of Middletown
        film crews in last election. Carey, portrayed more
        sympathetically in "The Campaign," nonetheless
        expresses more misgivings about experience than
        Wilson.

516.   "'Middletown': Another Wilson-Carey Match Shaping Up?"
        MUNCIE EVENING PRESS, 25 March 1982, p. 1.

        Notes local reaction to "The Campaign" generally
        positive. Interviews with Carey and Wilson, the two
        mayoral candidates, suggest rematch likely.

517.   North, Juli. "First of 'Middletown' Series Draws
        Positive Viewer Reaction." MUNCIE STAR, 25 March
        1982, p. 23.

        Informal poll shows favorable viewer opinion
        concerning "The Campaign." Points out that Carey
        was studied more intimately than Wilson.

518.   Hawes, G.K. "'Middletown' Cast Confronts Its Creator."
        MUNCIE STAR, 26 March 1982, pp. 1, 7.

        Reports on local PBS call-in show during which Davis
        fielded questions about Middletown film series.

519.   Lough, Larry. "'The Big Game' - Next in Middletown
        Series." MUNCIE STAR, 26 March 1982, pp. 1, 11.

        Describes various scenes from Middletown segment.

1982

520.   "Producer Davis Responds to Local 'Middletown'
        Critics." MUNCIE EVENING PRESS, 26 March 1982,
        p. 12.

        Notes that most questions directed toward Davis
        during call-in show focused on "Seventeen," which
        was still in limbo regarding its airing or
        distribution.

521.   Terhune, Bill. "If You Like Basketball, You'll
        Love 'Big Game.'" MUNCIE EVENING PRESS, 26 March
        1982, pp. 1, 12.

        Provides highlights of segment, featuring matchup
        between Muncie Central and Anderson high schools.

522.   "Magazine and Group May Sue 'Middletown.'" MUNCIE
        EVENING PRESS, 27 March 1982, p. 2.

        Notice that "Seventeen" magazine and the Community
        of Praise religious group threaten to sue PBS over
        titles of two segments of Middletown series.

523.   Carlson, John. "'Middletown' Blew It When the
        Cameras Failed to Catch Me." MUNCIE EVENING PRESS,
        27 March 1982, p. 16.

        Recounts humorous, futile attempts to get into
        Middletown series.

524.   Emerson, Gloria. "Muncie Business." Nation 234
        (27 March 1982): 379-381.

        Reviews "The Campaign" and "Family Business"
        segments of Middletown series, finding them touching
        and noting commonality of pizza man Howie Snider and
        candidate Jim Carey as men with "outrageous and
        stubborn insistence on living intensely."

1982

525.   Olinger, Mary Ann. "'The Big Game' Is a Study
        of Hoosier Hysteria Here." MUNCIE EVENING PRESS, 27
        March 1982, p. T-2.

        Notes airing of part two of Middletown series on
        March 31, followed by local panel discussion.

526.   Shores, Larry. "'Middletown' Bits and Pieces."
        MUNCIE STAR 27 March 1982, sec. C, p. 6.

        Reflects upon critical praise but low ratings for
        first episode of Middletown series. Also notes
        disclaimers, from Lynd to Davis, about use of term
        "typical" in their work.

527.   Lehmann-Haupt, Christopher. "'Middletown' Producer's
        Book About Hamilton, Ohio, a 'Dramatic Story.'"
        MUNCIE STAR, 28 March 1982, sec. B, p. 4.

        Reprint of New York Times News Service story (see
        item 490).

528.   Clarke, Gerald. "Back Home in Indiana." TIME,
        29 March 1982, pp. 66-67.

        Reviews Middletown film series, finding "Family
        Business" poignant but "Seventeen" merely
        disagreeable. Criticizes cinema verite technique
        for failing to put episodes into perspective and
        also for subjecting viewers to frequent trite and
        boring scenes.

529.   Waters, Harry F. "Pulse of the Heartland." NEWSWEEK,
        29 March 1982, pp. 50-51.

        Reviews Hometown and Middletown film series, noting
        Davis' search for drama, as well as data, departs
        from Lynds' approach. Finds series powerful but
        questions whether camera's presence significantly
        altered behavior of subjects.

1982

530.   LaGuardia, Joan D.   "TV Producer Withdraws Controversial
        'Seventeen.'"   MUNCIE EVENING PRESS, 30 March 1982,
        p. 1.

        Account of Peter Davis' decision not to accede to
        PBS request to edit "Seventeen" segment further
        before airing. Also includes extensive discussion
        of local criticism to segment, as voiced by attorney
        for Muncie Community Schools.

531.   "As You Can See Our Students Are Perfect Angels."
        BALL STATE DAILY NEWS, 31 March 1982, p. 4.

        Editorial cartoon on Muncie Southside students and
        administrator after cancellation of "Seventeen."

532.   Emerson, Paul H.   "Hickstown, U.S.A."   MUNCIE STAR, 31
        March 1982, p. 4.

        Letter to editor by ex-resident of Muncie,
        expressing dismay over portrayal of community in
        "The Campaign."

533.   "Good Example."   MUNCIE STAR, 31 March 1982, p. 4.

        Letter to editor praising sportsmanship and maturity
        shown by Muncie's two mayoral candidates in "The
        Campaign."

534.   Hawes, G.K.   "'Middletown' Director Withdraws
        'Seventeen' from PBS Series."   MUNCIE STAR, 31 March
        1982, pp. 1, 5.

        Examines reasons not to edit or air "Seventeen" and
        includes comments by Davis, Muncie Community Schools
        officials and PBS executives.

1982

535.   Inman, Julia. "'Seventeen' Program Will Not Air."
        INDIANAPOLIS STAR, 31 March 1982, p. 15.

        Chronicles efforts to cancel segment of Middletown
        series, noting Indianapolis PBS general manager's
        comment that burying one's head in the sand
        (regarding teenagers' lives) may not be appropriate
        response.

536.   Mayer, Jane. "Producer Pulls Show Off Public
        Television Rather Than Cut It: Episode of
        'Middletown' Stirs Muncie, Ind., Delegation Over Sex
        and Drug Scenes." WALL STREET JOURNAL, 31 March
        1982, p. 35.

        Recounts Davis' difficulties with PBS, Xerox, and
        Muncie residents over airing of "Seventeen."

537.   Miller, Casey. "Davis Cancels Controversial
        'Seventeen.'" BALL STATE DAILY NEWS, 31 March 1982,
        p. 1.

        PBS announces withdrawal of segment, saying that
        Davis had option to edit to meet PBS' program and
        practices standards, but declined. Local comments
        concerning cancellation largely favorable.

538.   "Segment Canceled." BALL STATE DAILY NEWS, 31 March
        1982, p. 4.

        Editorial, dismayed that PBS withdrew "Seventeen."
        Suggests they bowed to local conservative pressure
        that couldn't handle harsh reality depicted in
        segment.

539.   Schwartz, Tony. "Final PBS 'Middletown' Segment
        Is Withdrawn." NEW YORK TIMES, 31 March 1982,
        sec. C, p. 29.

        Discusses Peter Davis' decision not to air
        "Seventeen," noting issue of free speech by
        filmmakers versus informed consent by subjects, who
        are minors.

1982

540.   "Does Documentary Have a Future?" AMERICAN FILM
        7 (April 1982): 57-64.

        Special report on long-standing debate revived by
        Middletown film series. Includes partial transcript
        of conference with participants such as Tom Brokaw,
        Theodore Caplow, Peter Davis and Richard Lingeman.

541.   Hawes, G.K. "Coach Didn't Like PBS's 'The Big Game.'"
        MUNCIE STAR, 1 April 1982, p. 27.

        Muncie Bearcat coach, Bill Harrell, feels Middletown
        film crew was intrusive. Also upset with handling of
        incident where three members of team suspended.

542.   Terhune, Karen. "Religion Segment of PBS Series Focuses
        On 1 Family." MUNCIE EVENING PRESS, 1 April 1982,
        p. 1.

        "Community of Praise," part three of the Middletown
        film series, focuses on lives and beliefs of a
        fundamentalist family. Community of Praise
        religious group threatening lawsuit over use of its
        name.

543.   Barnet, Bob. "'The Big Game' - Honest Picture." MUNCIE
        STAR, 2 April 1982, p. 13.

        Agrees with Middletown filmmakers that, in Indiana,
        basketball was appropriate subject for segment,
        particularly classic rivalry between Muncie Central
        Bearcats and Anderson Indians. Reflects upon various
        scenes, including interview session following film.

544.   Dahlin, Robert. "PW Interviews: Peter Davis."
        PUBLISHERS WEEKLY 221 (2 April 1982): 8-9.

        Davis explains different documentary styles used in
        Hometown (Hamilton, Ohio) book and Middletown Film
        Series, both released on same day.

1982

545.   Francisco, Brian. "Fundamentalist Christians 'Star' in
       Next PBS Episode." MUNCIE STAR, 2 April 1982, pp.
       1, 12.

       Focuses largely on interview with Phyllis Tobey and
       her experiences in filming "Community of Praise."

546.   "Name's Still the Same, but Now It's Disclaimed."
       MUNCIE STAR, 2 April 1982, pp. 1, 12.

       Notes disclaimer to be used in airing "Community of
       Praise" segment of Middletown series since same name
       also used by another ecumenical Christian group
       based in Muncie.

547.   Olinger, Mary Ann. "'Community of Praise' Examines a
       Muncie Family Relying on Faith." MUNCIE EVENING
       PRESS, 3 April 1982, T-2.

       Notes airing of part three of Middletown series on
       April 7, to be followed by local panel discussion.

548.   McDowell, Edwin. "More Exposure." NEW YORK TIMES BOOK
       REVIEW, 4 April 1982, p. 34.

       Advance notice of publication of Middletown Families
       and All Faithful People.

549.   O'Connor, John J. "When a Documentarian Tries to Play
       Sociologist." NEW YORK TIMES, 4 April 1982, sec. 2,
       p. 27.

       Critical review of PBS's Middletown series, alleging
       producer Davis has failed to see that life, values
       and social structures in Midwest have changed.
       Brief history of verite form of film documentation.

550.   Olinger, Mary Ann. "'Middletown' Notes Religious
       Side of Muncie." MUNCIE STAR, 4 April 1982, p. T-4.

       Overview of "Community of Praise" segment of
       Middletown series, with examination of Tobey
       family's religious beliefs.

1982

551.   Toth, Susan Allen. "In Search of Middle America."
       NEW YORK TIMES BOOK REVIEW, 4 April 1982, p. 9.

       Review of HOMETOWN, noting that Davis more
       interested in presenting instances of tension and
       crisis than quiet routine. Still, praises his
       storytelling abilities, which make Hamilton, Ohio
       come alive.

552.   Unger, Arthur. "PBS's Canceled 'Middletown' Segment:
       Was Its Slice of Life Spiced Up?" CHRISTIAN SCIENCE
       MONITOR, 5 April 1982, p. 16.

       Questions tendency of cinema verite form of
       filmmaking, to encourage subjects to perform in
       front of camera, and to use editing process to
       emphasize filmmaker's point of view. Believes that
       "Seventeen" "does a disservice to the youngsters
       involved, the city of Muncie, and also the
       filmmakers."

553.   "'Middletown' No!" MUNCIE EVENING PRESS, 6 April
       1982, p. 5.

       Letter to editor, criticizing Middletown film
       series.

554.   Terhune, Bill. "'Middletown' Films - A Plus for
       the City." MUNCIE EVENING PRESS, 6 April 1982,
       p. 4.

       Summarizes national media coverage of Middletown
       film series, and offers personal assessment that it
       has been a great success.

555.   Hawes, G.K. "Church Leader Sees Third 'Middletown'
       Segment in Good Light." MUNCIE STAR, 8 April 1982,
       p. 29.

       Interviews Marcus Haggard, featured in "Community of
       Praise." Describes appeal of charismatic,
       pentecostal movement for people with problems,
       searching for answers.

1982

556.   Olinger, Mary Ann. "'Family Business' Shows Muncie
        Family Work to Save Pizza Parlor." MUNCIE EVENING
        PRESS, 10 April 1982, p. T-2.

        Notes airing of part four of Middletown series on
        April 14, to be followed by local panel discussion.

557.   Olinger, Mary Ann. "'Family Business' to Air on
        'Middletown'." MUNCIE STAR, 11 April 1982, p. T-3.

        Brief overview, noting scenes were shot from
        December 1980 through February 1981.

558.   Sheppard, Nathaniel, Jr. "Muncie Finds Film on
        Students a Distorted Mirror." NEW YORK TIMES, 12
        April 1982, sec. A, p. 16.

        Interviews attorneys representing Southside High
        School and students involved in "Seventeen" segment
        of Middletown series. Emphasizes Muncie's family-
        oriented community structure and local disbelief of
        film's authenticity.

559.   "About Middletown Series on PBS." MUNCIE EVENING
        PRESS, 13 April 1982, p. 6.

        Reports mixed reactions from six "men-on-the-
        street."

560.   Terhune, Bill. "Middletown? Why, That's Normal
        City." MUNCIE EVENING PRESS, 13 April 1982, p. 4.

        Tongue-in-cheek letter to editor, claiming that
        Normal City (suburb of Muncie) would have been
        better site than Muncie for film series.

561.   Douglas, Donna. "Talk of the Town." MUNCIE STAR,
        14 April 1982, p. 9.

        Includes announcement on arrival of Theodore
        Caplow's MIDDLETOWN FAMILIES at area bookstores.
        Notes Caplow visiting Muncie, 27 April 1982, to talk
        about book.

1982

562. Yaeger, Don. "'Middletown' Focuses on Shakey's
      Family." BALL STATE DAILY NEWS, 14 April 1982,
      p. 3.

      Describes how Snider family chosen as representative
      for family and work sections of PBS Middletown
      series. Howard Snider also discusses filming
      process and shares his opinion concerning film.

563. Hermansen, Vicki. "'Family Business' Stars Enjoy
      Their Segment." MUNCIE STAR, 15 April 1982,
      pp. 1, 6.

      Reports on Snider family seeing themselves for first
      time in Middletown series segment. Whole family, in
      rare move, took time off from pizza business.

564. Orr, Eloise. "Snider Family Gets 'Hang in There' Calls
      from all Over Country." MUNCIE EVENING PRESS, 16
      April 1982, p. 1.

      Subjects of "Family Business" recount tremendous
      response to segment, much of it from other
      struggling small business owners.

565. Hermansen, Vicki. "Business Is Booming: Howie Snider
      Says 'Middletown' Series Has Changed His Life."
      MUNCIE STAR, 17 April 1982, sec. B, p. 1.

      Snider discusses nationwide telephone calls,
      donations and increased business resulting from
      airing of "Family Business."

566. Olinger, Mary Ann. "'Second Time Around' Looks at a
      Couple Planning Future." MUNCIE EVENING PRESS, 17
      April 1982, p. T-2.

      Notes airing of part five of Middletown series on
      April 21, to be followed by local panel discussion.

1982

567.   Barnet, Bob. "All Together Now: Let's Be Typical."
        MUNCIE STAR, 18 April 1982, sec. A, p. 12.

        Suggests that Muncie is weary of being butt of
        jokes, subject to yet another "inspection of our
        crankshafts with the suspicion that there may be
        cracks." Still, on balance, finds Middletown film
        series a careful and accurate portrayal.

568.   Davis, Peter. "Hometown, U.S.A.: Pride and Prejudice in
        America." FAMILY WEEKLY, 18 April 1982, pp. 6-8.

        Describes search that led to Hamilton, Ohio as site
        for HOMECOMING, published concurrently with airing
        of Middletown film series.

569.   Herbers, John. "How They're Doing in Muncie, Ind."
        NEW YORK TIMES BOOK REVIEW, 18 April 1982,
        pp. 11, 30.

        Review of MIDDLETOWN FAMILIES with findings about
        persistence of family and religious beliefs.
        Wonders about status of underclass in Muncie. Also
        critical of writing by committee approach and
        delayed analysis and publication of data from the
        study.

570.   Caplow, Theodore. "The Myth of Family Decline -
        and Its Benefits." CHRISTIAN SCIENCE MONITOR, 19
        April 1982, p. 23.

        Argues that sociological myth of declining family is
        comforting to those who find their own situation
        better than the "average" or "typical" family in
        crisis.

571.   LaGuardia, Joan D. "PBS 'Middletown' Series
        Looks at Remarriage." MUNCIE EVENING PRESS, 21
        April 1982, p. 2.

        Summary of "Second Time Around," also updating
        relationship of Elaine Ingram and David Shesler, now
        married.

1982

572.   Conn, Earl L. "Now and Then a Story Comes from
        the Heart." MUNCIE WEEKLY NEWS, 22 April 1982,
        p. 6.

        Discusses dozens of phone calls to Snider family
        after airing of "Family Business." Many calls from
        small businessmen sympathizing with Snider's plight.

573.   Francisco, Brian. "'Middletown' Pair Splitting."
        MUNCIE STAR, 22 April 1982, p. 1.

        Reports filing of dissolution of marriage petition
        by Phillip and Phyllis Tobey, featured in "Community
        of Praise."

574.   Hawes, G.K. "'The Second Time Around' or Marriage in
        Muncie, Ind." MUNCIE STAR, 22 April 1982, pp. 1, 6.

        Producer/director Davis provides background on
        filming of Middletown series segment and principal
        subjects, David Shesler and Elaine Ingram, react
        positively to experience.

575.   "'Middletown' Book Available." MUNCIE STAR, 22 April
        1982, p. 5.

        Notes Caplow's visit to Ball State, coinciding with
        release of MIDDLETOWN FAMILIES. Includes brief
        summary of research methodology and findings.

576.   Carlson, John. "Now the Sniders Are Shaky Over
        Possible TV Show." MUNCIE EVENING PRESS, 23 April
        1982, p. 2.

        Notes that Henry Winkler interested in making
        "Family Business" a television series.

577.   Hawes, G.K. "Sniders' 'Family Business' May Be
        Basis of TV Series." MUNCIE STAR, 23 April 1982,
        pp. 1, 9.

        Examines Henry Winkler offer to adapt Middletown
        segment for television series.

1982

578.   "Middletown Lecture Slated at BSU Monday."
        MUNCIE STAR, 24 April 1982, sec. A, p. 6.

        Notes forthcoming second annual Center for
        Middletown Studies lecture, "Middletown as a
        Literary Document," by Richard Lingemam.

579.   "More 'Middletown' Set Next Week." MUNCIE
        EVENING PRESS, 24 April 1982, p. T-1.

        Outlines week of Middletown-related activities,
        including lectures by Theodore Caplow and Richard
        Lingeman.

580.   Olinger, Mary Ann. "'Middletown Revisited'
        Looks at Muncie Research." MUNCIE EVENING PRESS, 24
        April 1982, p. T-2.

        Notes airing of part six of Middletown series on
        April 28. Program moderator and host Ben Wattenberg
        examines Middletown studies, including film series,
        in Muncie PBS affiliate WIPB-TV's first nationally
        televised production. Shown in time slot initially
        reserved for "Seventeen."

581.   Cole, Ben. "'Middletown' Has Beseiged Sharp's Staff."
        MUNCIE STAR, 25 April 1982, sec. B, p. 7.

        Notes that U.S. Rep. Philip R. Sharp's office has
        been inundated with inquiries since airing of
        Middletown film series.

582.   Creech, Floyd A. "Reaction to 'Middletown' Mostly
        Favorable." MUNCIE STAR, 25 April 1982, p. 9.

        Notes numerous calls and letter from around country
        in response to Middletown film series. Most positive
        but some ex-Muncie residents embarrassed.

1982

583.   Spurgeon, Bill. "'Middletown Families': The Work of
       Caplow and His Organization Follows Lynd Studies
       Faithfully as Possible." MUNCIE STAR, 25 April
       1982, sec. B, p. 4.

       Compares detailed replication techniques of
       Middletown III researchers to "slice of life"
       approach of Middletown film series which does not
       attempt to provide "typical" view of Middletown
       behavior. Also reflects upon flurry of interest by
       national media, often resulting in superficial
       accounts.

584.   Coldwater, Charles F., M.D. "The Typical American City
       Blues." MUNCIE STAR, 26 April 1982, p. 4.

       Satirical poem, expressing severe indecision until
       Middletown III studies tell him how to think and
       act.

585.   Baur, Michael. "Muncie Considered 'Alternate
       Lifestyle.'" MUNCIE STAR, 27 April 1982, p. 3.

       Summarizes talk by Richard Lingeman, who argues
       current migration from large cities to smaller
       towns, a facet of national decentralization process.

586.   "Editor Explains Success of 'Middletown' Studies." BALL
       STATE DAILY NEWS, 27 April 1982, p. 1.

       Nation editor, Lingeman, notes in Ball State lecture
       that Lynds' Middletown made city dwellers more aware
       of small-town lifestyles.

587.   LaGuardia, Joan D. "Researcher Talks on Middletown
       50 Years Later: 'Family, Religion Have Changed
       Little Here.'" MUNCIE EVENING PRESS, 27 April 1982,
       p. 1, 14.

       Recounts week of Middletown-related activities,
       including Caplow talk on "The Future of Religion in
       Middletown." Notes Caplow was student of Lynd and
       discussed Middletown studies with him.

1982

588.   Graham, Christina. "Author Addresses Meeting:
        Surveys Show City 'Less Religious.'" BALL STATE
        DAILY NEWS, 28 April 1982, p. 1.

        Caplow, summarizing findings of ALL FAITHFUL PEOPLE
        at Ball State's Friends of Bracken Library annual
        meeting, notes that church attendance has increased,
        overall devoutness decreased, and new religious
        tolerance evident.

589.   North, Juli. "Increased Tolerance Noted in Muncie
        Churches." The MUNCIE STAR, 28 April 1982, p. 5.

        Speaking to Friends of Bracken Library, Caplow
        discusses greater tolerance and higher level of
        religious practice than time of Lynd studies.

590.   Terhune, Karen. "Tonight the 'Middletown' Series
        Is Examined." MUNCIE EVENING PRESS, 28 April 1982,
        p. 1.

        Discusses "Middletown Revisited" hosted by Ben
        Wattenberg. Contrasts Middletown III researchers'
        statistical approach and Middletown filmmakers'
        decision to focus on crisis and controversy, rather
        than "representative" situations.

591.   Hawes, G.K. "'Middletown Revisited' Helps Put
        Series in Perspective." MUNCIE STAR, 29 April 1982,
        p. 22.

        Focuses on Wattenberg interviews with producer Peter
        Davis, series participants such as Howie Snider,
        community leaders such as State Representative
        Hurley Goodall, and Middletown III researcher
        Theodore Caplow.

592.   Yeager, Don. "Censorship Holding the Truth." BALL STATE
        DAILY NEWS, 29 April 1982, p. 4.

        Criticizes WIPB-TV station manager Needham and
        Channel 49 support of "Seventeen" censorship
        efforts.

1982

593.   Baur, Michael. "Panelists Project Muncie in Year 2000."
        MUNCIE STAR, 30 April 1982, pp. 1, 2.

        "Muncie 2000" panelists argue Middletown studies
        focus on past and present, to exclusion of future.
        Predict Muncie in year 2000 as center of haves and
        have-nots.

594.   Stodghill, Dick. "See Here Now, This Isn't Middletown
        and We Ain't Hicks." MUNCIE EVENING PRESS, 30 April
        1982, p. 2.

        Tongue-in-cheek account of conversation with old
        newspaper buddies about Muncie's ill-deserved
        reputation as city of rubes.

595.   Condran, John G., and Jerry G. Bode. "Rashomon,
        Working Wives, and Family Division of Labor:
        Middletown, 1980." JOURNAL OF MARRIAGE AND THE
        FAMILY 44 (May 1982): 421-26.

        Data from random sample of 316 currently married
        Middletown adults suggests wives still perform most
        household tasks, regardless of work status. Also
        finds evidence of "Rashomon effect" that husbands
        and wives differ significantly in perception of
        degree of household assistance offered by husband.

596.   Douglass, Joanne. "Another View of 'Middletown.'" ARTS
        INSIGHT 44 (May 1982): 30-31.

        Middletowner reflects upon Davis' film series,
        finding local criticism more offensive than some of
        rougher scenes in "Seventeen." Suggests that Muncie,
        rather than expecting Chamber of Commerce portrayal,
        might learn something from views shown in series.

597.   "'Middletown' Conclusions." MUNCIE STAR, 2 May 1982,
        sec. A, p. 12.

        Editorial commenting favorably on Ben Wattenberg's
        followup segment to Middletown film series.

1982

598.   O'Connor, John J. "TV: 'The Letter' by Maugham."
        NEW YORK TIMES, 3 May 1982, sec. C, p. 18.

        Review of upcoming programs includes discussion of
        "Middletown Revisited," hosted by Ben Wattenberg,
        which replaces originally scheduled "Seventeen."

599.   McGrath, Ellie. "The Fat Boy in the Canoe." TIME,
        10 May 1982, pp. 102-3.

        Describes National Endowment for the Humanities
        Chairman William J. Bennett's funding priorities --
        more emphasis on traditional humanities projects
        such as bibliographies, and fewer television
        programs such as PBS Middletown series.

600.   Synovitz, Ron. "Shakey's Benefits from TV Segment."
        BALL STATE DAILY NEWS, 12 May 1982, p. 3.

        Howie Snider explains filming process for "Family
        Business" and its impact on his enterprise, after
        special showing of film at Ball State.

601.   Nordell, Roderick. "In Mid-America, Researchers See
        Family Values Holding Strong." CHRISTIAN SCIENCE
        MONITOR, 14 May 1982, sec. B, p. 3.

        Review of MIDDLETOWN FAMILIES and HOMETOWN, finding
        Caplow study more analytical and persuasive, while
        Davis' treatment more sensational, with similarities
        to TV docudramas.

602.   Elder, Glen H. "A Third Look at Middletown." SCIENCE
        216 (21 May 1982): 854-57.

        Review of MIDDLETOWN FAMILIES, generally positive
        but questions whether central thesis that family
        decline is a myth itself is creating another myth of
        "ever harmonious, successful family life."

1982

603.   Greene, Dick. "Seen and Heard in Our Neighborhood."
        MUNCIE STAR, 25 May 1982, p. 4.

        Reflects upon Robert Lynd's visits to Muncie and his
        personal contacts with Lynd.

604.   Caplow, Theodore. "Religion in Middletown." THE PUBLIC
        INTEREST 68 (Summer 1982): 78-87.

        Research report summarizing themes of increased
        tolerance and vitality of traditional religion, to
        be analyzed at greater length in forthcoming ALL
        FAITHFUL PEOPLE.

605.   Barron, Milton L. "The Jews of California's Middletown:
        Ethnic vs. Secular Social Services." JEWISH SOCIAL
        STUDIES 44 (Summer-Fall 1982): 239-54.

        Characterizes Fresno as "Middletown" of California
        communities, in which Jews comprise middle-size
        subcommunity. Examines needs and problems,
        particularly regarding social services, in such
        areas where there is general rapid growth and
        concurrent increase in Jewish population.

606.   Bahr, Howard M. "Shifts in The Denominational
        Demography of Middletown, 1924-1977." JOURNAL FOR
        THE SCIENTIFIC STUDY OF RELIGION 21, June 1982:
        99-114.

        Compares 1920s/1930s and latter 1970s data, noting
        increase of Southern Protestantism (mainly Baptists
        and Pentacostal-evangelical churches) and sustained
        participation in organized religion.

607.   Caplow, Theodore. "Christmas Gifts and Kin Networks."
        AMERICAN SOCIOLOGICAL REVIEW 47 (June 1982): 383-92.

        Argues that ritualized gift giving in Middletown
        society "is a way of reinforcing relationships that
        are highly valued but insecure."

1982

608.   Johnson, Steven [sic] D., and Joseph B. Tamney.
        "The Christian Right and the 1980 Presidential
        Election." JOURNAL FOR THE SCIENTIFIC STUDY OF
        RELIGION 21 (June 1982): 123-31.

        Finds, after interviewing Middletown residents, that
        strongest Reagan support not from Christian Right
        but highly educated conservatives. Religious
        fundamentalism not seen as major factor in American
        politics.

609.   Rodman, Howard. "Muncie's Blackboard Jungle."
        AMERICAN FILM 7 (June 1982): 10, 12, 14.

        Traces controversy surrounding "Seventeen" segment
        of Middletown series and eventual decision to
        withdraw it from PBS schedule.

610.   Nemerowicz, Gloria. Review of MIDDLETOWN FAMILIES.
        LIBRARY JOURNAL 107 (1 June 1982): 1106.

        Emphasizes authors' replicative techniques and their
        findings of continuity in values and institutions.

611.   Fox, Richard. "The Missing Community in Middletown."
        IN THESE TIMES, 2-15 June 1982, pp. 20-21.

        Review of PBS film series, arguing that overwhelming
        concentration on personal and family issues leads to
        neglect wider issues of community life in America.

612.   Lingeman, Richard. "Muncie Protects Its Own." NATION
        234 (12 June 1982): 722-27.

        Examines attempts by Muncie residents to prevent
        showing of "Seventeen" and finds Middletown film
        approach to cinema verite lacking in sociological,
        journalistic and aesthetic context.

1982

613.   Long, Doug. "WIPB-49 Issued Reprimand." BALL
         STATE DAILY NEWS, 16 June 1982, p. 1.

         WIPB-TV (Muncie PBS affiliate) accused of censorship
         by Indiana Associated Press Broadcasters
         Association. WIPB and general manager Needham seen
         as important forces in cancellation effort against
         "Seventeen."

614.   "'Seventeen' Protest Draws Fire from Hoosier AP
         Broadcasters." MUNCIE EVENING PRESS, 19 June 1982,
         p. T-4.

         Note on IAPBA resolution criticizing WIPB actions
         leading up to cancellation of "Seventeen." Signed
         by IAPBA president, Jack McQuate, public affairs
         director of WBST, Ball State radio station.

615.   Elliott, Peg. "Those Dirty Words." MUNCIE STAR,
         26 June 1982, sec. A, p. 6.

         Expresses disapproval regarding Davis' choice of
         school and main characters in "Seventeen." Considers
         segment "slap in the face" for those who have helped
         educate the "good kids."

616.   "Album of Yesteryear." MUNCIE STAR, 27 June 1982,
         sec. C, p. 12.

         Photo of Bourke-White, while she photographed Muncie
         City Council meeting for LIFE article (see item 96).

617.   "Veterinarian J.M. Haggard Dies During Visit to NYC."
         MUNCIE STAR, 20 July 1982, p. 1.

         Reports that founder and developer of International
         Charismatic Ministry, Dr. Marcus Haggard, suffered
         heart attack at religious conference in New York
         City. Haggard was featured in "Community of Praise"
         segment of Middletown film series.

1982

618.   Hawes, G.K. "There'll Be More Questions for
        Inhabitants of 'Middletown.'" MUNCIE STAR,
        11 August 1982, p. 1.

        Middletown III researcher Howard Bahr discusses
        mailing of leisure activities questionnaire and
        projected results.

619.   Baur, Michael. "From Pizza to TV: Howie Snider
        Ready to Sign Hollywood Contract." MUNCIE STAR, 13
        August 1982, pp. 1, 14.

        Contract offers from television and major motion
        picture producers announced by Snider at press
        conference. Notes Middletown series' nominated for
        Emmy in outstanding informational series category.

620.   Hewitt, John D., Eric D. Poole, and Robert M. Regoli.
        "Felony Case Disposition Patterns in Middletown,
        1932-1975." CRIMINAL JUSTICE REVIEW (Fall 1982):
        58-67.

        Analyzes data from criminal court dockets, finding
        that felony prosecution and convictions lagged
        behind rise in reported crime, plea bargaining
        became increasingly popular, "role of court
        appointed defense counsel changed dramatically...,
        time delays between filing of information and
        sentencing increased greatly after the mid-1960s...,
        and sentences to state penal institutions declined."

621.   Vander Hill, Warren. "The Middletown Film
        Project: Reflections of an 'Academic Humanist.'"
        JOURNAL OF POPULAR FILM AND TELEVISION 10 (Autumn
        1982): 48-65.

        Describes development of project, as one of Ball
        State professors to initiate the idea. Criticizes
        lack of historical/sociological perspective shown in
        final film segments.

1982

622.   Review of MIDDLETOWN FAMILIES. Choice 20
        (October 1982): 353.

        Offers background on Middletown studies and
        Middletown III researchers, noting this is first of
        three projected volumes.

623.   Kenney, Anne. "History Professor Questions
        'Middletown' Findings." BALL STATE DAILY NEWS, 28
        October 1982, p. 5.

        Ball State history professor, Dwight Hoover,
        disagrees with Lynds' contention that religion dies
        out during times of social tension. Will pursue
        this argument in paper to be presented to
        Tocqueville Society.

624.   Caplow, Theodore. "Decades of Public Opinion:
        Comparing NORC and Middletown Data." PUBLIC OPINION
        5 (October/November 1982): 30-31.

        Argues that National Opinion Research Center and
        Middletown survey data (from Lynds to Middletown
        III) show relatively high stability and satisfaction
        with personal situations, but more volatile shifts
        and discontent regarding public issues.

625.   Cherlin, Andrew. "Middletown III: The Story Continues."
        CONTEMPORARY SOCIOLOGY 11 (November 1982): 617-19.

        Review of MIDDLETOWN FAMILIES, praising replication
        concept but critical of upbeat tone, seemingly not
        always squaring with findings such as high divorce
        rates.

626.   Janis, Ralph. "Middletown Revisited: Searching
        for the Heart of Mid-America." INDIANA MAGAZINE OF
        HISTORY 78 (December 1982): 346-51.

        Review of Middletown film series, finding it a
        personal and moving view of lower-middle class
        lives, but arguing need to provide context and
        assessment.

1983

627.   Caplow, Theodore, et al. ALL FAITHFUL PEOPLE: CHANGE
        AND CONTINUITY IN MIDDLETOWN'S RELIGION.
        Minneapolis: University of Minnesota Press, 1983.

        Chapters by Theodore Caplow, Howard M. Bahr, Bruce
        A. Chadwick, Dwight W. Hoover, Laurence A. Martin,
        Joseph B. Tamney, and Margaret Holmes Williamson.
        Findings based primarily on Middletown III survey
        data, collected 1977-1981, much of which replicated
        earlier Lynd studies central thesis that pace of
        modernization slowing, and that persistence and
        renewal of religion characterize situation in
        Middletown more than secularization.

628.   Caplow, Theodore, and Bruce A. Chadwick.
        "Inequality and Life Styles in Middletown, 1920-
        1978." In NEW PERSPECTIVES ON THE AMERICAN FAMILY,
        edited by R. Warren and L. Lyon, 122-35. Homewood,
        Ill.: Dorsey Press, 1983.

        Reprint of item 349.

629.   Fox, Richard Wightman. "Epitaph for Middletown:
        Robert S. Lynd and the Analysis of Consumer
        Culture." In THE CULTURE OF CONSUMPTION CRITICAL
        ESSAYS IN AMERICAN HISTORY, 1880-1980, edited by
        Richard Wightman Fox and T.J. Jackson Lears,
        101-41. New York: Pantheon Books, 1983.

        Examines Middletown volumes in light of Lynd's
        progression from Christian minister to secular
        sociologist, from cultural analyst to political
        activist, from outsider to member of the
        professional elite, and from critic of American
        consumer capitalism to critic of irrational American
        consumer.

630.   Holmes, Marilou Judy. "A History of Professional
        Nursing Education in Middletown, 1906-1968."
        Ed.D. thesis, Ball State University, 1983.

        Traces development of nursing programs in Muncie,
        arguing they followed general American trends,
        ultimately leading to National League for Nursing
        and state accreditation.

1983

631.   Lynd, Helen Merrell, with the collaboration of
        Staughton Lynd. POSSIBILITIES. Rev. ed.
        Bronxville, N.Y.: Friends of the Esther Raushenbush
        Library, Sarah Lawrence College, 1983.

        Includes new introduction by Susanne Hoeber Rudolph
        and notes, in acknowledgements, that publication is
        part of effort to make available contents of Lynd's
        unpublished papers, held by college archives. See
        also item 276.

632.   Marvin, Grace Maria. "Community Bonds in
        Middletown: Re-Investigating the Concept and
        Correlates of Localism." Ph.D. diss. University of
        Virginia, 1983.

        Analyzes data from Government Services Survey
        of Middletown III Project, arguing that
        interpersonal bonds in local community continue in
        urban setting, contrary to assumptions of
        sociologists forecasting possible effects of the
        coming mass society.

633.   Silverman, Jonathan. FOR THE WORLD TO SEE: THE
        LIFE OF MARGARET BOURKE-WHITE. New York: Viking
        Press, 1983.

        Includes description of Middletown assignment, one
        picture from essay chosen for exhibition of American
        art at Musee du Jeu de Paume in Paris.

634.   Vander Hill, Warren. THE MIDDLETOWN FILM
        PROJECT: ONE YEAR LATER. A Talk Given to Friends of
        Alexander M. Bracken Library, 30 April 1983.
        Muncie, Ind.: Ball State University, 1983.

        Updated version of "Middletown Film Project..." (see
        item 621).

1983

635.   Bahr, Howard M., Theodore Caplow, and Bruce A. Chadwick.
        "Middletown III: Problems of Replication,
        Longitudinal Measurement, and Triangulation."
        ANNUAL REVIEW OF SOCIOLOGY 9 (1983): 243-64.

        Analyzes own replication techniques and offers
        typology of replicative studies, based on variables
        of time, place, method and subjects covered. Also
        suggests guidelines for future replicators.

636.   Lough, Larry. "The Year That 'Middletown' Made
        the Big Time." MUNCIE STAR, 2 January 1983, sec. A,
        p. 16.

        Year in review includes comments on Peter Davis'
        Middletown film series.

637.   "Campus Has Muncie Data in Computer." MUNCIE
        STAR, 23 January 1983, sec. B, p. 8.

        Ball State sociology professor, Harry Nelsen,
        explains that Middletown data retrieval system
        permits survey information search from Lynd studies
        to present departmental surveys to be retrieved.

638.   Bahr, Howard M., and Alexander E. Bracken. "The
        Middletown of Yore: Population Persistence,
        Migration, and Stratification." RURAL SOCIOLOGY 48
        (Spring 1983): 120-32.

        Argues that preindustrial Muncie was not the placid
        rural community depicted by Lynds. Instead, it
        exhibited rapid growth, high population turnover and
        concentrated wealth in hands of small elite.

639.   Hoover, Dwight W. Review of HOMETOWN. ANTIOCH
        REVIEW 41 (Spring 1983): 246.

        Notes that book and Middletown film series, both by
        Davis, share same conceptual framework used by
        Lynds. Does not find book successful, however, as
        sociology or as literature, despite attempts to
        emulate Sherwood Anderson's WINESBURG, OHIO.

1983

640.   Yencer, Rick. "Political Veteran, Newcomer File
        GOP Council Bids." MUNCIE STAR, 1 March 1983, p. 8.

        Notes that Elaine Shesler (PBS "Middletown" series,
        Second Time Around) seeking Republican nomination
        for council-at-large. Gives brief personal
        background.

641.   "Middletown Out-takes to BSU." MUNCIE STAR,
        13 March 1983, sec. B, p. 9.

        Notice of NEH grant to bring PBS Middletown series
        materials including 500 hours of film, to Muncie.

642.   Ringlespaugh, Mike. "University to Get
        Middletown Film Series." BALL STATE DAILY NEWS, 23
        March 1983, p. 3.

        Five segments of six-part PBS Middletown Film Series
        obtained by Ball State University, along with
        outtakes, notations and film logs. "Seventeen"
        episode not included.

643.   Harvey, Charles E. Review of ROBERT S. LYND
        SPECIAL ISSUE, THE JOURNAL OF THE HISTORY OF
        SOCIOLOGY. JOURNAL OF THE HISTORY OF THE BEHAVIORAL
        SCIENCES 19 (April 1983): 192-95.

        Summarizes arguments of many of the issue's
        articles, noting in particular that they shed new
        light on circumstances under which Lynds conducted
        their first study.

644.   Rapp, Rayna, and Ellen Ross. "It Seems We've
        Stood and Talked Like This Before: Wisdom from the
        1920s." MS., April 1983, pp. 54-56.

        Discusses 1920s backlash to feminist movement and
        rise of consumer-oriented society, citing Lynd's
        findings on impact of automobile and movies on youth
        culture of the era.

1983

645.   Tievant, Sophie. "Les etudes de 'communaute' et
        la ville: heritage et problemes." SOCIOLOGIE DU
        TRAVAIL 25 (April–June 1983): 243–56.

        Includes discussion of Lynd's work as part of
        historical overview of community studies.

646.   Samuelson, Robert J. "Blue–Collar, White–Collar
        Distinctions Are Blurring." LOS ANGELES TIMES, 7
        April 1983, sec. 2, p. 7.

        Notes that U. S. Department of Labor dropping blue-
        collar/white–collar designations. Examines
        MIDDLETOWN in discussion of use and eventual
        outdatedness of terms.

647.   "Religion Briefs." MUNCIE STAR, 9 April 1983,
        sec. A, p. 4.

        Announces six–Sunday lecture series focusing on
        religion in Middletown. Includes discussions of
        "Community of Praise," church architecture, public
        relations and general history.

648.   "TV Key Previews." MUNCIE STAR, 15 April 1983,
        p. 14.

        Notes airing of made–for–TV–movie about murdering of
        cast members in late night soap opera entitled
        "Middletown U.S.A."

649.   "At Ball State." MUNCIE STAR, 22 April 1983,
        p. 9.

        Announces forthcoming third annual Center for
        Middletown Studies lecture, "Falling into the
        Future: Middletown in Decline, by Ball State
        sociology professor, Harry Nelson."

1983

650.   "Infamous 'Seventeen' Segment Won't Be Shown at
        Exposition." MUNCIE STAR, 27 April 1983,
        p. 18.

        AP story that "Seventeen" dropped from "Banned Film"
        showing of International Film Exposition (Filmex)
        due to earlier legal problems with parental consent.
        Gives brief history of controversial film.

651.   "Legal Problems Ax Showing of 'Middletown'
        Film." BALL STATE DAILY NEWS, 27 April 1983, p. 1.

        AP story, same as item 650.

652.   Margulies, Lee. "U.S. Film Pulled from 'Banned
        Film' Series." LOS ANGELES TIMES, 27 April 1983,
        sec. 4, pp. 1, 8.

        Discusses pending litigation that led Davis to
        withhold consent for showing of "Seventeen," the
        U.S. entry, at Filmex series in Los Angeles.

653.   Bahr, Howard M., and Thomas K. Martin. "'And Thy
        Neighbor as Thyself': Self-Esteem and Faith in
        People as Correlates of Religiosity and Family
        Solidarity Among Middletown High School Students."
        JOURNAL FOR THE SCIENTIFIC STUDY OF RELIGION 22
        (June 1983): 132-44.

        Suggests, based on findings from 1977 Middletown III
        survey, that evangelical outlook or church
        attendance do not influence self-esteem. Church
        attendance, but not family solidarity, does have
        effect on faith in people.

1983

654.   Brodt, Stephen J., Dwight W. Hoover, and John D.
       Hewitt. "Policing Middletown: 1880-1900." JOURNAL
       OF POLICE SCIENCE AND ADMINISTRATION 11 (June 1983):
       237-42.

       Examines factors leading establishment of
       professional police force in 1893, and impact of
       police on community, most notably providing means to
       enforce higher standards of public behavior. Finds
       that charges for serious crimes already declining
       prior to creation of police force, but increase in
       charges for social order and vice crimes a result of
       more rigorous enforcement.

655.   Tamney, Joseph B., and Stephen D. Johnson. "The
       Moral Majority in Middletown." JOURNAL FOR THE
       SCIENTIFIC STUDY OF RELIGION 22 (June 1983): 145-57.

       Analyzes data from stratified, staged-random sample
       of 281 Muncie SMSA residents, finding Moral Majority
       supported by religious television influence,
       cultural fundamentalist attitudes and Christian
       Right advocacy.

656.   Fraser, Marie. "'Middletown' Out Takes Being
       Cataloged at BSU." MUNCIE STAR, 12 June 1983, sec.
       B, p. 8.

       Discusses NEH support to bring Middletown film
       series materials, with exception of "Seventeen," to
       Ball State where they will be added to Center for
       Middletown Studies collection data.

657.   Clark, Lindley H., Jr. "On the Road from Wall
       Street to Muncie." WALL STREET JOURNAL, 14 June
       1983, p. 37.

       Former Muncie resident reports on Ball State Center
       for Economic Education, focusing on usefulness of
       studying economy at local level rather than
       exclusively from perspective of Wall Street or
       Washington.

1983

658.   "Photo Show to Portray Middletown (1905-
        1935)." MUNCIE STAR, 29 June 1983, p. 21.

        Announces Ball State Art Gallery exhibit of
        photographs, grouped roughly according to themes
        explored by Lynds.

659.   Ringlespaugh, Mike. "Sociologist's Recent
        Study Should Dismiss Myths Resulting from Previous
        Research on Black Women." BALL STATE DAILY NEWS, 20
        July 1983, p. 1.

        Black Middletown researcher Vivian Gordon examines
        findings of interviews with 103 local black women,
        noting high degree of political activity but
        relatively low numbers in management, administration
        or professional positions. Argues, contrary to
        established literature, that most happy with role as
        wife and mother.

660.   "TV Crews to Film Muncie Couple's Church
        Activities." MUNCIE STAR, 23 July 1983,
        sec. A, p. 4.

        Reports NBC plans to film Rev. James Taylor and Rev.
        Barbara Shires-Taylor for "Monitor" program. Also
        will include scenes of other local religious
        activities.

661.   Gillette, Howard, Jr. "Middletown Revisited."
        AMERICAN QUARTERLY 35 (Fall 1983): 426-33.

        Review essay on MIDDLETOWN FAMILIES, HOMETOWN, and
        Middletown film series, contending none have lasting
        effect of Lynd studies. Argues over-dependence on
        survey data and unwarranted optimistic conclusions
        in MIDDLETOWN FAMILIES, failure to reach balance
        between social research and storytelling in
        HOMETOWN, an uneven results in film series although
        it "best exemplifies the Lynds' capacity to
        discipline a personal vision of American culture and
        give it artistic expression."

1983

662.   Winston, Brian. "Hell of a Good Sail... Sorry
        No Whales." SIGHT & SOUND, Autumn 1983,
        pp. 238-43.

        Review of Middletown film series, finding episodes
        "simplistic bastard form" of "direct cinema and
        cinema verite," abandoning any attempt at
        objectivity and interested in presenting ordinary
        folk only in extraordinary, crisis-ridden
        circumstances.

663.   LaForte, Robert S., and Richard Himmel, eds.
        "Middletown Looks at the Lynds: A Contemporary
        Critique by the Reverend Dr. Hillyer H. Straton of
        Muncie, Indiana, 1937." INDIANA MAGAZINE OF HISTORY
        79 (September 1983): 248-64.

        Reproduces manuscript held in Alvin M. Owsley
        Collection at North Texas State University and
        provides biographical information on Straton.

664.   Hitchens, Christopher. "American Notes." TIMES
        LITERARY SUPPLEMENT, 23 September 1983,
        p. 1020.

        Draws attention to poems of Charles F. Coldwater
        (see items 274 and 355) who chronicles lives of
        Middletowners and describes the Lynds, somewhat
        facetiously, as "mythical researchers in a fabulous
        lost town."

665.   Spurgeon, Wiley. "'All Faithful People' Study
        Detects Changes in Style, not in Substance of
        Religion in Muncie." MUNCIE STAR, 9 October 1983,
        sec. B, p. 4.

        Review of ALL FAITHFUL PEOPLE, noting conclusion
        that religion still plays important role in
        community, despite some changes in practice since
        Lynd studies.

1983

666.   Sargent, Thomas A. "Religion Now Stronger in
        Muncie: Caplow Survey Repeats 'Middletown'
        Questions." MUNCIE EVENING PRESS, 13 October 1983,
        p. 21.

        Review of ALL FAITHFUL PEOPLE, summarizing findings
        but warning their representativeness regarding
        status of religion in rest of country should not be
        overstated.

667.   Shores, Larry. "Seen and Heard in Our
        Neighborhood." MUNCIE STAR, 18 October 1983, p. 4.

        Review of NBC News' "First Camera" (formerly
        "Monitor") segment on religion in Middletown,
        praising segment's objectivity but criticizing
        neglect of Jewish community and portrayal of
        fundamentalist movement as dominant in Muncie.

668.   Shores, Larry. "Seen and Heard in Our
        Neighborhood." MUNCIE STAR, 27 October 1983, p. 4.

        Reports that poems by local resident Charles
        Coldwater (pseud.) included in TIMES LITERARY
        SUPPLEMENT article on Middletown, by Christopher
        Hitchens (see item 664).

669.   "Books: Christian Revivals." TIMES HIGHER
        EDUCATION SUPPLEMENT (London), 11 November 1983,
        p. 16.

        Review of ALL FAITHFUL PEOPLE, focusing on increase
        in number of churches, regularity of attendance,
        religious marriage ceremonies, and level of
        donations to religious institutions.

670.   Wood, Suzanne W. Review of ALL FAITHFUL PEOPLE.
        LIBRARY JOURNAL 108 (15 November 1983): 2167.

        Summarizes research results, noting substantial
        change since Lynd studies but "trend toward stronger
        religious affiliation and commitment."

1983

671.   Andrews, Samuel D., Robert R. Sherman, and Rodman
        B. Webb. "Teaching: The Isolated Profession."
        JOURNAL OF THOUGHT 18 (Winter 1983): 49-57.

        Draws on Lynd studies in discussion of low-paying,
        low-status teaching profession.

672.   Hoover, Dwight W., John D. Hewitt, and Jack
        Kirchner. "Crime and Mental Illness in Middletown,
        1870-1910: A Study in Social Control." INDIANA
        SOCIAL STUDIES QUARTERLY 36 (Winter 1983-84): 33-44.

        Describes local efforts to control social deviance
        during period of rapid industrial growth, focusing
        on differential treatment according to gender.

673.   Caplow, Theodore. "Response to the Comment by
        Miller and Cisin - Avoiding Bias in Derivative
        Samples: A Neglected Issue in Family Studies."
        AMERICAN SOCIOLOGICAL REVIEW 48 (December 1983):
        876.

        Concurs with Miller and Cisin's argument regarding
        weighting of derivative samples (see item 675).

674.   Harvey, Charles E. "Robert S. Lynd, John D.
        Rockefeller, Jr., and 'Middletown.'" INDIANA
        MAGAZINE OF HISTORY 79 (December 1983):
        330-54.

        Chronicles Lynd's difficulties with Institute of
        Social and Religious Research during period of
        initial Middletown study, arguing much of it due to
        Lynd's criticism of business class. Also argues
        against Richard Jensen's criticism of Lynds'
        methodological approach (see item 352).

1983

675.   Miller, Judith Droitcour, and Ira H. Cisin.
        "Avoiding Bias in 'Derivative Samples': A Neglected
        Issue in Family Studies." AMERICAN SOCIOLOGICAL
        REVIEW 48 (December 1983): 874-76.

        Argues "need for corrective weights in derivative
        samples," although acknowledging the bias in Caplow
        "Christmas Gifts and Kin Network" study may not have
        produced serious distortions. (see item 673 for
        Caplow's response).

676.   Caplow, Theodore, and Bruce A, Chadwick. "Six
        Decades of American Religion." COMMONWEAL 110 (2
        December 1983): 649-54.

        Excerpted from ALL FAITHFUL PEOPLE (see item 627).

1984

677.   Ball, Edmund F. "The Decade of the Twenties."
        In THE MIDDLETOWN PHOTOGRAPHS, 26-31. Muncie,
        Indiana: Center for Middletown Studies, Ball State
        University, 1984.

        As member of X-family, reflects upon changes in
        Middletown since 1920s, particularly growth of
        unions. Notes, interestingly, that none of X-family
        members apparently ever were contacted by Lynds.

678.   Caplow, Theodore. "Looking for Secularization
        in Middletown." In RELIGION: NORTH AMERICAN STYLE,
        edited by Patrick H. McNamara, 104-11. 2d ed.
        Belmont, Cal.: Wadsworth Publishing Company, 1984.

        Reprint of item 436, with additional bibliography.

1984

679.   Foster, Frank. "Photography: A Credible
        Messenger." In THE MIDDLETOWN PHOTOGRAPHS,
        9-12. Muncie, Indiana: Center for Middletown
        Studies, Ball State University, 1984.

        Explores historical importance of the "hack
        photographer" in documenting the local community.

680.   Gordon, Whitney H. "The Poetics of Sociology."
        In THE MIDDLETOWN PHOTOGRAPHS, 16-18. Muncie,
        Indiana: Center for Middletown Studies, Ball State
        University, 1984.

        Finds images in exhibition evocative but often more
        intrusive in what is not present or
        underrepresented, such as blue-collar Middletown.

681.   Hermansen, David R. "Visual Images of Muncie."
        In THE MIDDLETOWN PHOTOGRAPHS, 19-25. Muncie,
        Indiana: Center for Middletown Studies, Ball State
        University, 1984.

        Argues that exhibition's images document strikingly
        Middletown's manmade environment in the 1920s, from
        thriving central business district to marked
        residential growth of area surrounding teacher's
        college (supported by Lynds' X-family).

682.   Hoover, Dwight W. "As Seen on the Streets of
        Muncie." In THE MIDDLETOWN PHOTOGRAPHS, 13-15.
        Muncie, Indiana: Center for Middletown Studies, Ball
        State University, 1984.

        Focuses on treatment of window displays by
        commercial photographers in 1920s and notes Lynds'
        comments on mania for promotion during that era.

683.   THE MIDDLETOWN PHOTOGRAPHS. Muncie, Indiana:
        Center for Middletown Studies, Ball State
        University, 1984.

        Catalog of exhibit at Ball State Art Gallery,
        running May 20 - June 24, 1984.

1984

684.   Pettifer, Julian, and Nigel Turner. AUTOMANIA:
        MAN AND THE MOTOR CAR. Boston: Little, Brown and
        Co., 1984.

        Chapter entitled "Car Crazy" explores impact of
        automobile on American society, drawing examples
        from Lynds' Middletown studies.

685.   Sargent, Thomas A. "Introduction" to THE
        MIDDLETOWN PHOTOGRAPHS, 7-8. Muncie, Indiana:
        Center for Middletown Studies, Ball State
        University, 1984.

        Includes background information on photographic
        collections represented and organization of the
        exhibition.

686.   Spurgeon, Wiley W., Jr. MUNCIE & DELAWARE
        COUNTY: AN ILLUSTRATED RETROSPECTIVE. Woodland
        Hills, Cal.: Windsor Publications, 1984.

        Includes local reactions to Middletown studies, and
        photograph of Margaret Bourke-White with local
        municipal officials, during visit to do LIFE
        article.

687.   Whyte, William Foote. LEARNING FROM THE FIELD:
        A GUIDE FROM EXPERIENCE, pp. 38-39. California: Sage
        Publications, Inc., 1984.

        Presents Lynds' work as one of several examples in
        chapter entitled "Planning the Project and Entering
        the Field." Notes that local informants led Lynds
        to examine role of X-family in much greater depth in
        MIDDLETOWN in Transition and suggests that they
        might have realized X-family's influence more
        clearly in first study if they had conducted their
        research in more open manner.

1984

688.   Coenen-Huther, Jacques. "Observation et
        conceptualisation en sociologie: pour une
        epistemologie postive." REVUE DE L'INSTITUT DE
        SOCIOLOGIE (Universite de Bruxelles) 1/2 (1984):
        167-98.

        Examines Lynd studies as early examples of
        participant-observer approach in sociology.

689.   Edmonds, Anthony O. "Middletown: A Community
        Reacts to Social Science." PROCEEDINGS OF THE
        INDIANA ACADEMY OF THE SOCIAL SCIENCES, 1984, pp.
        87-93.

        Cites numerous responses, mostly in local
        newspapers, to various Middletown-related studies.
        Although some defend studies, many tired of
        attention or exasperated by frequent portrayal as
        "rubes and hicks."

690.   Smith, Mark C. "Fifty Years of an American City:
        Stability and Change in Middletown." INDIAN JOURNAL
        OF AMERICAN STUDIES 14, 1 (1984): 57-66.

        Traces Middletown studies from Lynds to Caplow,
        describing their examination of change and
        continuity as significant exception to usual
        ahistorical approach of social sciences.

691.   Berger, Peter L. "I Look Upon the World as My
        Parish." AMERICA 150 (21 January 1984):
        36-37.

        Review of ALL FAITHFUL PEOPLE, noting relatively
        little religious change in Middletown, although more
        tolerance than before. Discusses the importance of
        study to recent secularization theory.

692.   Roof, Wade Clark. "Religiosity in Middletown."
        SCIENCE 223 (17 February 1984): 691.

        Review of ALL FAITHFUL PEOPLE, focusing on authors'
        contention that secularization is largely a myth in
        contemporary America.

1984

693. Trembley, David. Review of ALL FAITHFUL PEOPLE.
      CHRISTIAN CENTURY 101 (22 February 1984): 204.

      Short notice, emphasizing findings that Middletown
      more religious than 50 years ago.

694. "Historian Dwight Hoover Will Direct BSU Center
      For Middletown Studies." MUNCIE STAR,
      26 February 1984, sec. C, p. 9.

      Biographic sketch and description of Center's
      research agenda, including plans to attract scholars
      from variety of disciplines.

695. Tamney, Joseph B. "A Quantitative Analysis of
      Religious Ritual in Middletown: A Research Note."
      SOCIOLOGICAL ANALYSIS 45 (Spring 1984): 57-64.

      Examines responses from 112 of 217 Middletown
      churches, to develop instrument of measure for study
      of ritual. States that "...the variety of
      Middletown rituals suggest the need for a
      dimensional rather than a typological approach."

696. Review of ALL FAITHFUL PEOPLE. CHOICE 21 (March
      1984): 992-93.

      Notes that Middletown III replication of Lynd
      studies has led researchers to suggest that
      secularization may be a myth.

697. Trimberger, Ellen Kay. "Middletown Revisited:
      From Class Politics to Politics of the Family."
      THEORY AND SOCIETY 13 (March 1984): 239-47.

      Review of MIDDLETOWN FAMILIES, critical of authors
      "hopeful" approach and questioning their
      definitional acceptance of "family" being "only
      constituted through legal marriage of a heterosexual
      couple."

1984

698.   "Hoover to Direct Center for Middletown
        Studies." BALL STATE ALUMNUS 41 (5 April 1984): 3.

        Describes plans of Ball State professor, Dwight
        Hoover, to foster Middletown research, utilizing
        growing collection of resource materials.

699.   Carman, John. "PBS Made Wise Move in Deep-
        sixing 'Seventeen.'" ATLANTA CONSTITUTION,
        11 April 1984.

        Agrees with decision not to air "Seventeen,"
        although not manner in which matter was handled.
        Finds film moving but too provocative for diverse
        television audience.

700.   Covino, Michael. "Missing: The Strange Case
        of Seventeen." EXPRESS, 13 April 1984,
        pp. 10-12.

        Review of "Seventeen" prior to showing at Pacific
        Film Archive. Provides background on attempts to
        suppress film and is particularly critical of
        Vanderhill's account (see item 621) of filmmaking
        process.

701.   Weales, Gerald. "Welcome to Munciekin Land."
        NEW YORK REVIEW OF BOOKS 31 (26 April 1984): 43-45.

        Review of ALL FAITHFUL PEOPLE by wary native
        Hoosier, sensing complacency among Middletown III
        researchers. Wonders about disquiet lying beneath
        apparent facade of optimistic Middletown lives.

702.   Caplow, Theodore. "Rule Enforcement without
        Visible Means: Christmas Gift Giving in Middletown."
        AMERICAN JOURNAL OF SOCIOLOGY 89 (May 1984):
        1306-23.

        Analyzes findings from 1979 random sample of 110
        residents, concluding that gift giving follows
        unwritten, often unconscious, rules designed to deal
        with important but insecure relationships.

1984

703.   Fraser, Marie. "Middletown Photographs in
       Art Gallery Exhibition." THE MUNCIE STAR,
       13 May 1984, sec. B, p. 6.

       Describes exhibit based upon work of local
       commercial photographer, W.A. Swift. Photos taken
       in 1920s and early 1930s, when Lynds were doing
       Middletown studies.

704.   Johnson, Stephen D., and Joseph B. Tamney.
       "Support for the Moral Majority: A Test of a Model."
       JOURNAL FOR THE SCIENTIFIC STUDY OF RELIGION 23
       (June 1984): 183-96.

       Findings from Fall 1982 survey of 284 Middletown
       residents indicate that "Christian Right
       orientation, cultural ethnocentrism, and
       authoritarianism had a major impact on Moral
       Majority support. Respondent's education and age,
       and religious television had a secondary influence."

705.   Marty, Martin E. Review of ALL FAITHFUL PEOPLE.
       JOURNAL OF AMERICAN HISTORY 71 (June 1984): 156.

       Argues, despite Middletown findings, that religious
       fervor in many places signals a "new intolerance."

706.   Tamney, Joseph B., and Stephen D. Johnson.
       "Religious Television in Middletown." REVIEW OF
       RELIGIOUS RESEARCH 25 (June 1984): 303-13.

       Analyzes data from 1981 stratified, random sample of
       281 Middletown residents, finding Christian Right
       attitudes and religious fundamentalism are
       significant variables affecting frequency of
       watching conservative evangelists, but no evidence
       that opportunity influences viewing patterns.

1984

707.   Mannheimer, Steve. "Ghosts of 'Middletown'
        Return in Ball State Gallery Exhibition."
        INDIANAPOLIS STAR, 17 June 1984,
        sec. E, p. 10.

        Critique of photographic exhibit of Muncie in the
        1920s.

708.   Roof, Wade Clark. "Religion and Ethics."
        CONTEMPORARY SOCIOLOGY 13 (July 1984): 507-509.

        Includes review of ALL FAITHFUL PEOPLE, questioning
        its dismissal of hypothesis of secularization in
        America.

709.   Towler, Robert. "Muncie Revisited." TIMES
        LITERARY SUPPLEMENT (LONDON), 6 July 1984,
        p. 765.

        Review of ALL FAITHFUL PEOPLE, summarizing
        three major changes since Lynd studies: lines of
        religious demarcation, blurred, increased religious
        participation, and less strenuous religious demands.

710.   Benson, Sheila. "Seventeen." LOS ANGELES TIMES,
        7 July 1984, sec. 5, p. 8.

        Brief review for Filmex showing, finding segment a
        "must-see" and noting vivid intimacy of filmmakers
        with their subjects.

711.   Schroeder, W. Widick. Review of ALL FAITHFUL
        PEOPLE. CHICAGO THEOLOGICAL SEMINARY REGISTER 74
        (Fall 1984): 39-41.

        Finds some unevenness of style due to multiple
        authorship, but concurs with generalizations about
        continuity and change, and notes wealth of detail,
        "utilizing interviews, questionnaires, archival
        research, participant observation, and secondary
        historical sources."

1984

712.   Metzger, Juli North. "Schools Hope to Stop Film
        Showing." MUNCIE STAR, 3 November 1984, p. 1.

        Discusses local school corporation efforts to block
        "Seventeen" showing at Washington film festival on
        grounds of violating privacy rights of students
        appearing in film.

713.   Metzger, Juli North. "Washington Audience Views
        'Seventeen.'" MUNCIE STAR, 4 November 1984, sec. A,
        p. 17.

        Notes showing of "Seventeen" at Kennedy Center,
        despite objections of local school officials.

714.   Surrey, Peter J. "Muncie Today: Has Sociology
        Changed Its Mind about Christianity?" LIVING
        CHURCH, 25 November 1984, pp. 11-12.

        Argues tendencies of influential sociological works,
        including Lynd studies, to be hostile to religious
        belief but Middletown III research, particularly in
        more sympathetic approach.

715.   Caplow, Theodore. "Social Criticism in Middletown:
        Taking Aim at a Moving Target." QUALITATIVE
        SOCIOLOGY 7 (Winter 1984): 337-39.

        Responds to Smith's "From MIDDLETOWN to Middletown
        III" (see item 716), suggesting that differences in
        findings of studies may be due to shifts in
        characteristics of society rather than perspectives
        of researchers.

1984

716.   Smith, Mark C. "From MIDDLETOWN to Middletown
        III: A Critical Review." QUALITATIVE SOCIOLOGY 7
        (Winter 1984): 327-36.

        Contends that Caplow and associates indicate
        relative lack of social change in Muncie and
        generally praise community's institutions, but such
        conclusions stem from their uncritical acceptance of
        survey data and fail to question quality of life.
        Concludes that "in so doing, they have abandoned the
        Lynds' perspective of the outside, critical observer
        and joined the chorus of self-satisfied
        Middletowners."

717.   Fichter, J.H. Review of ALL FAITHFUL PEOPLE.
        REVIEW OF RELIGIOUS RESEARCH 26 (December 1984):
        192-93.

        Summarizes Middletown III findings, noting present-
        day Muncie residents may be more religious than
        predecessors but, according to Gallup and NORC data,
        less pious than national norm. Also cautions reader
        about Middletown's label of "typicality" and
        authors' generalizations regarding measurement of
        secularity.

718.   Rogers, Richard L. Review of ALL FAITHFUL
        PEOPLE. JOURNAL FOR THE SCIENTIFIC STUDY OF
        RELIGION 23 (December 1984): 420.

        Sees book as "...a polemic against the widely-
        disseminated idea of secularization," but argues
        authors have not fully explained relationship
        between social and religious change.

1985

719.   Caplow, Theodore. "Christmas Gifts and Kin
        Networks." In FAMILY STUDIES REVIEW YEARBOOK, 1985,
        edited by B.C. Miller and D.H. Olson, 467-76.
        Beverly Hills: Sage, 1985.

        Reprint of item 607.

720.   Caplow, Theodore. "Christmas Gifts and Kin
        Networks." In READINGS IN SOCIOLOGY, edited by
        B. Vargas. Acton, Mass.: Copley Publishing Group,
        1985.

        Reprint of item 607.

721.   Hewitt, John D., and Dwight W. Hoover. USERS
        GUIDE TO "MY GRANDFATHER'S MIDDLETOWN: THE CITY AND
        CULTURE IN THE TWENTIES." Muncie, Indiana: Center
        for Middletown Studies, Ball State University, 1985.

        Includes individual descriptions for slide show,
        discussion questions and suggestions for related
        activities.

722.   Hickey, Eric W. "Theoretical Paradigms: An
        Application of Functionalism and Conflict Theory to
        Religion in Middletown, U.S.A., 1924-1978." Ph.D.
        diss., Brigham Young University, 1985.

        Compares Middletown III data to that of Lynds,
        finding religiosity and religious behavior strong or
        stronger. Functionalism, more than conflict theory,
        helps explain change in religious behavior.

723.   Park, Jan Carl. Review of "Seventeen." NEW YORK
        NATIVE, 28 January-10 February 1985.

        Short note on "Seventeen" showing at Film Forum in
        New York, with quote on film from L.A. TIMES.

1985

724.   Canby, Vincent. "Screen: 'Seventeen,' A
        Documentary." NEW YORK TIMES, 6 February 1985, sec.
        C, p. 19.

        Reviews commercial release of "Seventeen," finding
        it a disturbing and provocative depiction of
        American life.

725.   Connelly, Sherryl. "A Teen Movie without the
        Games and Guffaws." DAILY NEWS (New York), 6
        February 1985.

        Describes "Seventeen" as a shocking documentary
        about teens who will not escape the future their
        class has prescribed for them.

726.   Winsten, Archer. "Not So Sweet 'Seventeen.'"
        NEW YORK POST, 7 February 1985.

        Views "Seventeen" not as entertainment, but rather
        as jarring vision of contemporary American youth.

727.   White, Armond. "Seventeen's a 10!" CITY
        SUN, 13-19 February 1985, p. 17.

        Describes film as tragedy, compelling society to
        view end of adolescence realistically, not
        romantically.

728.   Salamon, Julie. "At the Movies: The Kids Are
        All Right." THE WALL STREET JOURNAL,
        14 February 1985, p. 28.

        Describes "Seventeen" as "disturbing portrait of
        aimlessness," differing from other teenage films
        because it contains no "coming of age" celebration.

729.   Review of "Seventeen." VOICE, 19 February 1985,
        p. 76.

        Short note on Film Forum's run of "Seventeen."

1985

730.   Pasternak, Judith. "She Learned the Truth at
        Seventeen." GUARDIAN (New York), 20 February 1985,
        p. 19.

        Review of "Seventeen" showing at Manhattan's Film
        Forum. Notes vitality of film's characters but
        finds film technically deficient and poorly edited.

731.   Canby, Vincent. "Growing Up Misunderstood in
        Today's America." NEW YORK TIMES,
        24 February 1985, sec. 2, pp. 21, 24.

        Finds "Seventeen" a haunting example of direct
        cinema, particularly when compared with
        prefabricated Hollywood youth films such as
        "Breakfast Club," "Vision Quest," and "Streets of
        Fire."

732.   Morrone, John. "Everywhere, U. S. A." NEW YORK
        NATIVE, 25 February - 10 March, 1985.

        Review of "Seventeen," finding it realistic but
        discouraging in its portrayal of teenagers with
        little future.

733.   Smith, Mark C. "Rejoinder to Theodore Caplow."
        QUALITATIVE SOCIOLOGY 8 (Spring 1985): 63-64.

        Argues that Caplow's response (see item 715) to
        Smith's article "From MIDDLETOWN to Middletown III"
        (see item 716) fails to answer Smith's main
        contention that Middletown III data does not support
        optimistic conclusions drawn by Caplow and
        colleagues.

734.   Ventura, Michael. "Seventeen?" L.A. WEEKLY, 22-28
        March 1985.

        Hails "Seventeen" as significant in depiction of way
        working-class philosophy generates apathy and
        hopelessness in its youth.

1985

735.   Johnson, Stephen D. "Religion as a Defense in a
        Mock-Jury Trial." JOURNAL OF SOCIAL PSYCHOLOGY 125
        (April 1985): 213-20.

        Using "Middletown" residents and students as mock-
        jurors in child-abuse trial, finds that defense
        portraying accused as religious did not increase
        sympathy, as might be expected in a conservative,
        largely Christian community.

736.   Miller, Donald. Review of ALL FAITHFUL PEOPLE.
        ANGLICAN THEOLOGICAL REVIEW 67 (April 1985): 210-12.

        Focuses on refutation of secularization myth, while
        noting strength of work lies in its replicative
        approach, comparing findings with Lynds'.

737.   Trojan, Judith. "Front Row Center." WILSON
        LIBRARY BULLETIN 59 (April 1985): 548-49, 574.

        Review of commercial version of "Seventeen," finding
        it disturbing and faulting filmmakers for their
        sensationalism.

738.   Bahr, Howard M., and Bruce A. Chadwick.
        "Religion and Family in Middletown, U.S.A." JOURNAL
        OF MARRIAGE AND THE FAMILY 47 (May 1985): 407-14.

        Summarizes Middletown III findings regarding
        persistence of family solidarity and religiosity,
        noting preliminary analysis also suggests two trends
        related but unclear in what manner.

739.   Metzger, Juli North. "'Seventeen' Is Still
        Packing Them in." MUNCIE STAR, 9 May 1985,
        pp. 1, 3.

        Notes "Seventeen" still receiving national and
        international recognition despite rejection by
        Muncie school officials.

1985

740.   "Despite Local Censoring, Other Cities See and
        Like 'Seventeen.'" MUNCIE EVENING PRESS,
        9 May 1985, p. 12.

        Describes critical acclaim at showings in several
        foreign countries and major cities across U.S.

741.   Shores, Larry. "Seen and Heard in Our
        Neighborhood." MUNCIE STAR,
        10 May 1985, p. 4.

        Note on Muncie couple who saw, "Seventeen" on
        television during stay in Hong Kong.

742.   Hillman, Ruth. "Seen and Heard in Our
        Neighborhood." MUNCIE STAR, 14 May 1985,
        p. 4.

        Southside High School teacher reflects upon
        "Seventeen," noting two of main characters were in
        her class. Suggests that much of their behavior was
        bravado, spurred on by camera's presence.

743.   "'Middletown' Premiere Planned for Thursday."
        MUNCIE STAR, 15 May 1985, p. 12.

        Note on slide/tape program entitled "My
        Grandfather's Middletown," which utilizes local
        photo collection in presenting history of 1920s
        Muncie.

744.   Terhune, Bill. "Why All the Fuss over
        'Seventeen'?" MUNCIE EVENING PRESS, 16 May 1985,
        p. 4.

        Sees "Seventeen" more as reflection of present
        permissiveness in our society, than exploitive,
        inaccurate film.

1985

745.   Morrissey, Charles T. "Oral History and the
        Boundaries of Fiction." PUBLIC HISTORIAN 7 (Spring
        1985): 41-46.

        Includes discussion of Middletown, in context of
        questioning why community identities are
        fictionalized by social scientists.

746.   Hoover, Dwight W. "To Be a Jew in Middletown:
        A Muncie Oral History Project." INDIANA MAGAZINE OF
        HISTORY 51 (June 1985): 131-58.

        Examines Muncie Jewish population primarily in
        1920s, noting high geographical mobility, restricted
        access to community life dominated by Christian
        values, and overt discrimination accentuated by Klan
        influence.

747.   Johnson, Stephen D., and Joseph B. Tamney.
        "Mobilizing Support for the Moral Majority."
        PSYCHOLOGICAL REPORTS 56 (June 1985): 987-94.

        Random sample of Middletown residents reveals
        support influenced by local church leaders, as well
        as conservative religious television.

748.   Tamney, Joseph B., and Stephen D. Johnson.
        "Consequential Religiosity in Modern Society."
        REVIEW OF RELIGIOUS RESEARCH 26 (June 1985): 360-78.

        Examines data from Autumn 1981 stratified, staged-
        random sample of 281 Middletown residents, finding
        religious influence greater in private than public
        realm, but some impact in all aspects of life among
        fundamentalists.

749.   Narcalli, Joseph A. Review of ALL FAITHFUL PEOPLE.
        JOURNAL OF THE AMERICAN ACADEMY OF RELIGION 53
        (June 1985): 295-96.

        Short summary of findings, also discussing
        relationship to Lynd studies.

1985

750.   Coldwater, Charles F. "Two Views." MUNCIE STAR,
        1 June 1985, sec. B, p. 8.

        Letter to editor, arguing that Muncie ban of
        "Seventeen" prevents community from forming unbiased
        opinions of the film.

751.   Buckley, William F. "Fleeing the Religious
        Right." MUNCIE STAR, 4 June 1985, p. 4.

        Discusses ALL FAITHFUL PEOPLE (see item 627) in
        context of reviewing "What the Fundamentalists Want"
        by Richard John Neuhaus.

752.   Spurgeon, Bill. "Seen and Heard in Our
        Neighborhood." MUNCIE STAR, 20 June 1985,
        p. 4.

        Discusses "My Grandfather's Middletown" slide show
        on Muncie in 1920s, produced by Ball State's Center
        for Middletown Studies.

753.   Gerhart, Lee. "Middletown Creator Prof. Lynd
        Returned." MUNCIE EVENING PRESS, 22 June 1985,
        p. 4.

        Looks back on Robert Lynd's arrival 50 years
        earlier, to do study of Middletown.

754.   Seay, Davin. "Teenage Troubles." CONTEMPORARY
        CHRISTIAN MAGAZINE, August 1985, p. 24.

        Review of three movies, including "Seventeen" which
        never aired on PBS but released as feature-length
        documentary. Finds its "unflinching depiction of
        alcoholism, sexual promiscuity, racism, and parental
        neglect" distressing and symptomatic of many
        teenagers.

1985

755.   White, Armond. "Kidpix." FILM COMMENT, August
       1985: pp. 9-15.

       Discusses themes and philosophies of teen movies,
       judging "Seventeen" more realistic and effective
       than others of same genre.

756.   Caplow, Theodore. "The Changing Balance of Work
       and Leisure in Middletown, 1924-1982." INDIANA
       SOCIAL STUDIES QUARTERLY 18 (Autumn 1985): 36-48.

       Reviews stratification literature, including Lynd
       studies, drawing distinction between social class
       and economic class. Argues that Muncie, with
       increased production, consumption and leisure,
       represents nearly socially classless society whereas
       economically classless society appears to be
       theoretically impossible "in any modern community
       that relies upon industrial production and the
       division of labor that is essential to industrial
       production."

757.   Frank, Carl M. "'Middletown' as a Model for
       Community Studies (with Comparative Data from Erie,
       Pennsylvania)." INDIANA SOCIAL STUDIES QUARTERLY 18
       (Autumn 1985): 7-24.

       Provides overview of Middletown studies, but
       suggests that some changes, such as growth of Ball
       State University, have made the community less
       representative. Argues instead that Erie, Penn-
       sylvania may provide more "appropriate barometer of
       the nation's culture."

758.   Hewitt, John D. "Patterns of Female Criminality
       in Middletown: 1900-1920." INDIANA SOCIAL STUDIES
       QUARTERLY 18 (Autumn 1985): 49-59.

       Finds increased involvement of females in property
       offenses, but decline in charges for sex-related
       offenses. Suggests that prostitution may not have
       decreased during time period but "use of criminal
       sanctions to control the behavior was changing."

1985

759.   Hoover, Dwight W. "Middletown's Religion:
        Faith in a Non-Ethnic Community." INDIANA SOCIAL
        STUDIES QUARTERLY 18 (Autumn 1985):
        60-70.

        Provides brief historical overview of Muncie
        religious groups and analyzes Lynds' methodology in
        MIDDLETOWN section on religion.

760.   Spaeth, Robert L. "Popular Theology." THIS
        WORLD no. 12 (Fall 1985): 129-32.

        Includes review of ALL FAITHFUL PEOPLE, finding it
        reliable, rather unexciting, and descriptive of
        cheerful, optimistic religion that not always
        evident elsewhere.

761.   Tamney, Joseph B., and Stephen D. Johnson.
        "Christianity and the Nuclear Issue." SOCIOLOGICAL
        ANALYSIS 46 (Fall 1985): 321-27.

        Survey results from sample of 393 Middletown
        residents indicate that Catholics, influenced by
        public stands of Catholic leaders, more likely to
        favor nuclear freeze than protestants.

762.   Turner, Nancy. "The Muncie Police Department:
        Origins to World War II (1893-1940)." INDIANA
        SOCIAL STUDIES QUARTERLY 18 (Autumn 1985): 71-90.

        Describes influence of changing local social and
        political milieu upon development of law enforcement
        in Middletown.

763.   Young, Lawrence A. and Bruce Chadwick.
        "Transience: Social Mobility In Middletown, 1890 to
        1979." INDIANA SOCIAL STUDIES QUARTERLY 18 (Autumn
        1985): 25-35.

        Argues that Middletown experienced transience or
        rapid social change during period of
        industrialization, from 1890 to mid 1920s, but
        adjustment to industrialization since then resulted
        in substantially slower rate of change.

1985

764.   White, Michael J. "Determinants of Community
        Satisfaction in Middletown." AMERICAN JOURNAL OF
        COMMUNITY PSYCHOLOGY 13 (October 1985): 583-97.

        Based upon survey of 220 respondents, examines
        variables such as perceived social support, cultural
        opportunities, services, community attractiveness
        and maintenance, pride in community, and sense of
        belonging, as major determinants of community
        satisfaction.

765.   Haddad, Anne Marie. "Teens' Slayings Shock
        Middletown, U.S.A." USA TODAY, 2 October 1985,
        sec. A, p. 8.

        Discusses murder in local park of Muncie, known for
        "textbook example of life in a typical USA
        community."

766.   Ward, Desiree. "Quality of 'Middletown U.S.A.'
        Life Queried Again by Sociology Group." BALL STATE
        DAILY NEWS, 15 October 1985, p. 3.

        Ball State professor, Dr. John Condran, heads
        sociology group devising 1985 telephone survey to
        determine quality of life in Muncie with regard to
        jobs, incomes, and relationships.

767.   Krebs, Michelle. "How the Auto Forever Changed
        Lives: The Story of Middletown, U. S. A."
        AUTOMOTIVE NEWS (Centennial Celebration Issue), 30
        October 1985, pp. 59-74.

        Cites Lynd studies extensively, noting impact of
        automobile on Middletown lives by 1920s, and
        summarizes more recent trends, including flight to
        suburb, decay of inner cities, decline of automotive
        industry and impact of increased gasoline prices.
        Concludes with guardedly optimistic view of the
        automobile in mid-1980s.

1985

768.   Barth, Ilene. "Middletown Revisited: Surprising."
        SARASOTA HERALD-TRIBUNE, 5 November 1985.

        Focuses on findings from MIDDLETOWN FAMILIES and ALL
        FAITHFUL PEOPLE, as described by Caplow at symposium
        sponsored by Library of Congress. Also cites
        national surveys tending to support Middletown III
        conclusions.

769.   Johnson, Stephen D., and Joseph B. Tamney. "The
        Christian Right and The 1984 Presidential Election."
        REVIEW OF RELIGIOUS RESEARCH 27 (December 1985):
        124-33.

        Data from random sample of 351 Middletown residents
        indicates that political/religious factors more
        influential in 1984 than 1980, but has backlash
        effect since more anti-Moral Majority than Moral
        Majority voters.

770.   Simpson, John H. "Socio-moral Issues and Recent
        Presidential Elections." REVIEW OF RELIGIOUS
        RESEARCH 27 (December 1985): 115-23.

        Argues, on basis of 1980 national sample and 1984
        Middletown sample, that New Christian Right has had
        indirect impact on recent presidential elections in
        the sense that orientations to social issues
        influence choices as voters.

1986

771.   Goldberg, Vicki. MARGARET BOURKE-WHITE: A
        BIOGRAPHY. New York: Harper & Row, 1986.

        Includes background on shooting of photographs
        appearing 1937 LIFE article (see item 96).

1986

772.   Hoover, Dwight W. MAGIC MIDDLETOWN.
        Bloomington, Ind.: Indiana University Press, in
        association with Historic Muncie, Inc., 1986.

        Pictorial history focusing primarily on 1920s, thus
        providing visual counterpoint to Lynds' sociological
        data. Title derived from "Magic City" appellation
        frequently applied to Muncie.

773.   Johnson, Stephen D. "The Christian Right in
        Middletown." In THE POLITICAL ROLE OF RELIGION IN
        THE UNITED STATES, edited by Stephen D. Johnson and
        Joseph B. Tamney, 181-98. Boulder, Colorado:
        Westview Press, 1986.

        Summarizes findings of series of Johnson and Tamney
        studies, 1980-84, which analyzed nature of support
        for Moral Majority and influence of Christian Right
        on 1980 and 1984 presidential elections.

774.   Johnson, Stephen D., and Joseph B. Tamney. "The
        Clergy and Public Issues in Middletown." In THE
        POLITICAL ROLE OF RELIGION IN THE UNITED STATES,
        edited by Stephen D. Johnson and Joseph B. Tamney,
        45-70. Boulder, Col.: Westview Press, 1986.

        Reports findings of 1984 Middletown clergy study,
        distinguishing between liberal and conservative
        factions. Notes that liberals theologically more
        homogenous than counterparts, but conservative
        churches more homogenous than liberal ones, since
        greater tendency for conservative ministers in
        liberal churches than vice versa.

775.   Moxley, Lucina Ball. RECOLLECTIONS OF LUCINA:
        THE BEST YEARS. Privately printed, 1986.

        Daughter of William H. Ball, featured on cover of
        LIFE issue with Bourke-White article photo-essay
        (see item 96), describes negative effects of Lynd
        studies on family's privacy and reputation. Talks
        about assignment as student journalist, interviewing
        Helen Lynd at Sarah Lawrence.

1986

776.   Rose, Irene Kathryn. "Testing Coalition Theory
        in THE GREAT GATSBY and the RABBIT Trilogy."
        Ph.D. diss., University of Oklahoma, 1986.

        Focuses on family changes from 1920s to 1960s,
        arguing increase in status for married women and
        decrease for married men. Draws upon Caplow's
        replication of Lynd studies for analysis of literary
        works.

777.   Kindt, Ann. "Early Middletown Women Dominated
        Artistic Scene." BALL STATE DAILY NEWS,
        21 January 1986, p. 7.

        Describes talk by visiting Center for Middletown
        Studies fellow, Andrew Yox, who finds influence of
        women on Muncie arts movement, 1889-1929, a
        reflection of changing sexual roles and
        expectations.

778.   Millard, Nancy. "Muncie Women Started Quite a
        Social Movement Here." MUNCIE STAR, 26 January
        1986, sec. B, p. 4.

        Summarizes Andrew Yox talk, "When Women Dominated
        the Arts: Music, Painting and Literature in
        Middletown."

779.   Goldsmith, Rae. "Satisfaction Found in Good
        Supply." MUNCIE STAR, 1 February 1986,
        sec. A, p. 14.

        Survey by Ball State sociologist, John Condran,
        indicates 55% satisfied with life in Muncie and 95%
        satisfied with marriages. Argues Muncie reflective
        of national trends though local residents "tend to
        be more conventional in their lifestyles."

1986

780.   Glenn, Norval D. Review of ALL FAITHFUL PEOPLE.
        AMERICAN JOURNAL OF SOCIOLOGY 91 (March 1986):
        1277-79.

        Charges that author's dismissal of secularization
        theory is premature not entirely supported by own
        data. Also notes that statistics on religiosity do
        not provide adequate measure of strength of
        conviction.

781.   Tamney, Joseph B. "Fasting and Dieting: A
        Research Note." REVIEW OF RELIGIOUS RESEARCH
        27 (March 1986): 255-62.

        Examines shifts in practice and meaning of fasting
        as indicators of religious change. Findings, based
        on 1977 Middletown III religion questionnaires,
        indicate present-day fasting mainly for secular
        reasons but some religious motivation, particularly
        among fundamentalists and charismatic christians.

782.   Newell, Michael. "Middletown Man's Musical Past
        Discovered." BALL STATE DAILY NEWS, 24 March 1986,
        p. 3.

        Rather belated review of 1964 record album "The
        Captains in Pensacola" of which Howie Snider,
        subject of Middletown segment "Family Business," was
        member.

783.   Kotlowitz, Alex. "Return to Middletown: Traditional
        Values and Changing Demographics Shape the Leisure
        Patterns of Middle America." WALL STREET JOURNAL,
        21 April 1986, sec. D, pp. 4, 7.

        Interviews several Muncie residents, concluding that
        leisure pursuits, with obvious exception of
        television, have not changed significantly since
        1920s. Business and working classes still don't mix
        much during free time, and basketball continues to
        reign supreme.

1986

784.   Kang, Xie. "Muncie - The Middletown of the
        United States." WORLD ECONOMIC HERALD, 26 April
        1986.

        Brief summary, in Chinese, by Shanghai special
        correspondent.

785.   Dennis, Rutledge. "The Black Middletown
        Journal." VCU MAGAZINE 15 (Summer 1986):
        10-14.

        Excerpts from journal entries made over the period
        from July to December, 1980. Author lived in "Black
        Middletown" to collect detailed information on
        various aspects of Black community life. Part of
        the larger study "Black Middletown: A Community
        Study of Social Process."

786.   Hoover, Dwight W. "Cocaine Use not a New Problem."
        MUNCIE STAR, 26 July 1986, sec. B, p. 12.

        Notes that problem persistent since early 20th
        century, with section of Muncie called "cocaine
        alley," but use of cocaine now found in better
        neighborhoods of America.

787.   Baer, Diane. "'Magic Middletown' Recalls 1920s
        in Muncie." MUNCIE EVENING PRESS, 11 September
        1986, p. 21.

        Favorable review of item 772.

788.   Koumoulides, John T.A. "Praise for Doc."
        MUNCIE STAR, 12 September 1986, p. 4.

        Letter to editor congratulates Charles F. Coldwater
        for being quoted in TIMES LITERARY SUPPLEMENT
        (London) article on Middletown.

1986

789.   Spurgeon, Bill. "'Magic Middletown' Sure to
        be a Collector's Item." MUNCIE STAR,
        21 September 1986, sec. B, p. 6.

        Favorable review of item 772.

790.   Baer, Diane. "Muncie Historian's Knowledge of
        His Adopted Home Is Well-known." MUNCIE EVENING
        PRESS, 25 September 1986, p. 9.

        Interviews Dwight W. Hoover, Director of Center for
        Middletown Studies, focusing on association with
        Middletown III and Middletown Film Project.

1987

791.   Caplow, Theodore. "Paretian Theory Applied to
        the Findings of the Middletown III Research." REVUE
        EUROPEENNE DES SCIENCES SOCIALES 25, 76 (1987):
        55-78.

        Relates theory of Vilfredo Pareto, regarding social
        change, to Middletown III data. From 1920s to 1980s
        finds an improvement but not equalization of income,
        and more equal distribution of level of education.

792.   Szopa, Anne. "Images of Women in Muncie Newspapers,
        1895-1915." Ph.D. diss., Ball State University,
        1987.

        Analyzes views of prostitution in Middletown and
        related distinctions between "good" and "fallen"
        women.

1987

793.   Hoover, Dwight W. "The Long Ordeal of Modernization
        Theory: Muncie as a Case Study." PROSPECTS (Spring
        1987): 407-51.

        Traces history and approaches to modernization
        theory, from nineteenth century German sociology to
        Middletown III studies. Responds to various
        criticisms of Middletown III findings regarding
        secularization and religiosity.

794.   Hoover, Dwight W. "The Middletown Film Project:
        History and Reflections." JOURNAL OF FILM AND VIDEO
        39 (Spring 1987): 52-65.

        Discusses background of Middletown film series,
        including ongoing tension between project humanists
        and producer Davis. Argues that filmmakers'
        adherence to direct cinema technique, with no
        voiceovers, talking heads or text, in final analysis
        meant that individual segments only captured surface
        of things and lacked both historical perspective and
        sociological insight.

795.   SOCIAL CHANGE REPORT.

        Quarterly newsletter for "large audience of opinion
        leaders seriously interested in the most recent
        research concerning contemporary social change in
        the Western world." Emphasis on Middletown-related
        topics. Editor, Theodore Caplow. Published by
        Center for Middletown Studies, Ball State
        University.

796.   Hewitt, John D., and Janet E. Mickish. "Prostitution
        During the Progressive Era: The Middletown
        Experience." WISCONSIN SOCIOLOGIST 24 (Spring-
        Summer 1987): 99-111.

        Argues that degree of social control exerted on
        prostitution was much greater in Middletown than
        larger cities of era, largely because "sexual
        services were regulated by town officials,
        officially through law and unofficially through
        corruption."

1987

797.   Johnson, Stephen D. "Factors Related to
        Intolerance of AIDS Victims." JOURNAL FOR THE
        SCIENTIFIC STUDY OF RELIGION 26 (March 1987):
        105-10.

        Survey of 371 Middletown residents reveals that
        supporters of Christian Right, advocating return to
        more traditional family life-style, tend to be
        prejudiced against homosexuals and hold intolerant
        attitudes toward AIDS victims.

798.   Gerhart, Lee. "Lynds' Report on Us Wasn't All
        Flattery." MUNCIE EVENING PRESS, 25 April 1987,
        p. 4.

        Notes how Muncie residents felt maligned by some of
        Lynds' assessments. Cites, in particular, Wilbur
        Sutton's response (see item 80).

799.   Gerhart, Lee. "Muncie Book Gave Critics a
        Feast." MUNCIE EVENING PRESS, 2 May 1987,
        p. 4.

        Reflects upon publication of MIDDLETOWN IN
        TRANSITION 50 years ago and summarizes reviews of
        work. Notes that, as a result of all the attention,
        "our town somewhat resembled a horse at an auction."

SUBJECT INDEX

175